Janisha Rondeau

MAKIN'
MINUTE COUNT !

By Cheryl Lavender

**Time-Savers, Tips,
And Kid-Tested
Strategies
For The
Music
Class**

EXCLUSIVELY DISTRIBUTED BY
HAL•LEONARD®
CORPORATION
7777 W. BLUEMOUND RD. P.O. BOX 13819 MILWAUKEE, WI 53213

Published by JENSON PUBLICATIONS
Exclusively distributed by HAL LEONARD PUBLISHING CORPORATION
P.O. Box 13819, 7777 W. Bluemound Rd.
Milwaukee, WI 53213 USA

Library of Congress Cataloging-in-Publication Data

Lavender, Cheryl.
    Making each minute count : time-savers, tips and kid-tested strategies for the music class / by
Cheryl Lavender.
        p.   cm.
    Includes bibiliographical references and index.
    ISBN 0-7935-0348-5 : $19.95
    1. School music – Instruction and study.   2. Music teachers – Time management.   I. Title.
MT1.L396 1990
372.87'044–dc20   90-22297
                                                                                                        CIP
                                                                                                         MN

Dedicated To

Tom and Gwen
my first teachers

ACKNOWLEDGEMENTS

I gratefully acknowledge the influence and inspiration of the following individuals who are unselfishly committed to nurturing the goodness in all children:

Elizabeth Brown — Author/Clinician; Assistant Professor of Music Education, Central Michigan University, Mt. Pleasant, MI

Emily Crocker — Editor/Composer/Clinician; Hal Leonard Publishing Corporation, Milwaukee, WI

Jim Fay — Author/Educator/Consultant - School Consultant Services, Inc. and Aurora University; Co-founder - Cline/Fay Institute: The Love and Logic People, Golden, CO

Susan Janscha — Private Piano Teacher, Brookfield, WI

Paul Lavender — Instrumental Publications Editor, Hal Leonard Publishing Corporation; Composer/Arranger/Clinician, Milwaukee, WI

Gregory Maass — Principal, Wisconsin Hills Elementary School, Brookfield, WI

Carolyn Mawby — Associate Professor of Music and Director of Choral Activities; Founder/Director of the Summer Academy of Music, University of Michigan, Flint, MI

Joanne Olsen — Watercolor and Fibre Artist/Illustrator/Author/Teacher, Thiensville, WI

Mary Pautz — Author/Clinician/Composer; Assistant Professor of Music Education, University of Wisconsin, Milwaukee, WI

Carol Wyrembelski — Elementary Band Director/Elementary Music Teacher; Private Teacher, French horn, Essexville, MI

Sister Lorna Zemke — Author/Clinician/Music Educator; Associate Professor of Music Education - Silver Lake College, Manitowoc, WI

Joe Amato (posthumously) — Author/Clinician; Special Education Teacher; Director - The Very Special Arts Festival, Fox Point, WI

TABLE OF CONTENTS

FOREWORD – REFLECTIONS FROM THE AUTHOR ix

CHAPTER 1:
ATTITUDE AND ATMOSPHERE – I MAKE THE DIFFERENCE 1
Effective Music Teaching 2
Healthy Self Concept 3
Positive Reinforcers 7
Word Power 9
Never A Wrong Answer 10
Special Times 11
The Sixth Sense 13

CHAPTER 2:
CLASSROOM MANAGEMENT AND DISCIPLINE – THE TEACHER/STUDENT RELATIONSHIP 15
Music Classroom Management 16
Acknowledging Appropriate Behavior 18
Dealing With Inappropriate Behavior – The C.Y.B. 22
The Musi-Contract 25
Simple Behavior Interventions 28

CHAPTER 3:
INCREDIBLY SUCCESSFUL TEACHING STRATEGIES – GENERAL TEACHING STRATEGIES 31
Thinking About Learning and Learning About Thinking 31
The Concept Chart 33

CHAPTER 4:
INCREDIBLY SUCCESSFUL TEACHING STRATEGIES – SPECIFIC TEACHING STRATEGIES

INCREDIBLY SUCCESSFUL TEACHING STRATEGIES – SPECIFIC TEACHING STRATEGIES 39

Strategies for Teaching *Beat* 39
Strategies for Teaching *Rhythm* 41
Strategies for Teaching *Meter* 50
Strategies for Teaching *Phrase* 58
Strategies for Teaching *Pitch and Melody* 59
Strategies for Teaching *Harmony* 67
Strategies for Teaching *Tempo* 70
Strategies for Teaching *Style* 71
Strategies for Teaching *Dynamics* 73
Strategies for Teaching *Tone Color* 77
Strategies for Teaching *Movement and Direction* 81
Strategies for Teaching *Form* 82
Strategies for Teaching *Interpretive Symbols* 83

CHAPTER 5:
ATTENTION GRABBERS – NO-FAIL FUNSTERS

ATTENTION GRABBERS – NO-FAIL FUNSTERS 87

Let's Pretend 87
Imagine That 90
Fun With Props 93
Teachable Tactics 99
It's All In The Way You Say It 103
Variations Of A Theme 104
Tin-Ear Tune-Up Time 107
Taking Turns 108
Movement And Direction 109

CHAPTER 6:
HELLO AND GOODBYE – PERSONALIZING YOUR MUSIC CLASS

HELLO AND GOODBYE – PERSONALIZING YOUR MUSIC CLASS 111

Ringing In The New Year 111
A Musical Hello 111
Hall-Way Shenanigans 113
Surprise 114
Follow The Leader 115
A Musical Good-bye 116
Stealing More Time 117

CHAPTER 7:
   MUSICAL WARM-UPS – MIND-BODY-VOICE.............121
Attitude Warm-ups..122
Motor Warm-ups...123
Posture Warm-ups...126
Breathing Warm-ups 127
Vocal Warm-ups 130

CHAPTER 8:
   INTRODUCING AND DIGESTING NEW SONGS –
   IDEAS THAT REALLY WORK 139
Introducing New Songs..139
20 Guidelines For Choosing And Introducing Songs To Very Young
   Or Special Needs Children..142
Digesting New Songs..144

CHAPTER 9:
   MUSICAL LEARNING OUTCOMES –
   ASSESSMENT METHODS...151
Shared Responsibility...151
Negative Learning Outcomes...163
Whole-Group Assessment Games 165

CHAPTER 10:
   MAKING THE MUSIC ROOM OUR OWN –
   PERSONALIZING THE MUSICAL EXPERIENCE...........179
Music Room Managers..180
Personalizing The Music Room...182

CHAPTER 11:
   BEYOND THE MUSIC ROOM – PUBLIC RELATIONS....187
Public Relations Within The School..188
Public Relations Outside The School...195

CHAPTER 12:
AWARDS, FORMS, DOCUMENTS, AND MORE 201

The Very Special Person Award 202

Music Award #1 203

Music Award #2 204

Applause...205

Sound Off/Music Students Really Measure Up 206

Chorus Members/Please Take Note 207

Letter Of Communication (Sample Format) 208

Music Planning Calendar 209

Daily Teaching Schedule 210

Musical Themes For Bulletin Boards 211

Vocal Audition Guide 212

Music Performance Planning Guide – Song Selection................................213

It's Showtime..214

Staff Communication Letter 215

Parent Permission Slip 216

Student Cummulative Profile (Lower Elementary) 217

Student Cummulative Profile (Upper Elementary).....................................218

News Bulletin 219

Curriculum Goals Summary 220

INDEX 221

BIBLIOGRAPHY...225

ABOUT THE AUTHOR 227

FOREWORD

From a grown-up's perspective, it's enlightening to "rewind" back to my childhood, and "play back" my first, live magic show. I remember being consumed with curiosity. My eyes hardly blinked as I tried to solve the mysteries created by the magician with each trick. I tried every logical way to mentally out-wit his craft, but he kept me wondering, and applauding his cleverness. I wanted more.

Today as a teacher of children, the "child" in me asks: How was it that this person could capture my undivided attention and hold it, with seemingly effortless skill on HIS part, and have ME doing all the thinking? Somehow, he tickled my imagination and I silently volunteered to become excited about paying attention. Although I learned nothing about successfully performing those magic tricks, I did learn something about becoming motivated to learn. Someone had found a way of turning my learning switch to "ON."

I continue to question: How can I give to my students what the magician gave to me? Is it possible for me to create an atmosphere of curiosity and excitement for my music students, in which they remain "spellbound," too? How can I turn their learning switches to "ON?"

Having been directed to teach from music curricula that resemble encyclopedias, I also began to question the feasibility of my students and me successfully reaching those hundreds of music goals in the mere two, half-hour music lessons per week, afforded by the school district. How could we ever realistically accomplish so much in so little time?

In a typical music curriculum, the course content for one year's worth of music study is usually more than what most students can accommodate in two. For example, in the fourth grade:

> "students learn concepts about melody, rhythm, form, harmony, timbre, dynamics, and tempo. They refine their playing skills on a wide variety of classroom instruments. They are exposed to music history and appreciation. They learn to sing in tune, sing in harmony, and compose music. They manipulate their bodies from simple movements to complex choreography. They socialize and follow instructions, and, sing the same words and breathe all at the same time as their fellow chorus members in concert. And, above all, it is expected that they WILL enjoy music."

After teaching ten frustrating years, and feeling perennially inadequate as a music teacher, I came to the conclusion that I'd HAVE to be a magician with a bag full of tricks to pull off this curriculum. Right? With a little magic, I could FIND time, STRETCH time, SAVE time, and MAKE more time to meet all these goals. Compelled to search for a more practical approach, I began asking other music teachers about their success in meeting all the curriculum goals in any given school year. It was then that I found out I had lots of company.

I asked more questions. As a teacher, is it not my purpose to lead students toward their own discovery of new information? Is it not a magician's role to entertain? What if the two roles were combined? Couldn't a music teacher use some of the magician's "tricks" to arouse and captivate his/her students, while at the same time use teaching skills to draw them closer to the information being sought? But, unlike a magician, couldn't a music teacher CONTINUE to lead students in the direction of new information until they finally discover it, so they feel as if they possess the ability to "figure out the trick" all by themselves?

Could the roles of music teacher and magician complement one another? The magician entertains with a multi-sensory approach using sight, hearing, speech, and touch. Likewise, a sensitive music teacher uses a multi-sensory teaching style to satisfy students' varied learning needs. Both the music teacher and the magician recognize that the more visually, aurally and kinesthetically stimulating the approach, the more active the response. It seemed to me that both roles were compatible.

So, for the next seven years, my lesson plans evolved from an entirely new point of view: Instead of outlining only WHAT I was to teach, I began outlining the WAY I was to teach. The focus for my students shifted from WHAT to learn, to HOW to learn. Lesson Plans came to be called "Lesson Preps" (preparations). The result — not only did my students cover more curriculum content than ever before, but also, my music lessons became exciting learning experiences, for both me and my students!

Short of supplying "how to" instructions for pulling a rabbit out of the piano, the bulk of this resource collection offers time-saving, student-tested tips, techniques, suggestions, strategies, philosophies and, reproducible pages that were borne of the desire to accomplish more musical teaching/learning in less time. The intent of this book is to place the "magic wand" that casts the "magic spell" of musical learning into your hand.

Use these ideas to get maximum student response in your minimum lesson time. Make each minute count by choosing and adapting musical activities that appeal especially to your teaching situation. And remember, the "illusion" that the teacher is doing all the work is just that – an illusion. In reality, the teacher is having fun stimulating students' brains to do all the thinking! A little "magic" really can go a long way!

Cheryl A. Lavender

Cheryl A. Lavender

Kids and Music

are made to be loved

1 ATTITUDE AND ATMOSPHERE

I MAKE THE DIFFERENCE

What happens to a child the moment he/she enters our music classroom? The question is crucial, because from the first moment, the stage is set for meaningful learning to happen or not happen. The attitudes which shape children's learning behaviors during the music lesson are as varied as the individuals who own them. And, of paramount importance is the teacher's attitude about children and music-making. The learning atmosphere created within the lesson, and nurtured by the music teacher impacts either positively or negatively on every child's motivation and ability to learn and perform. This means that, for meaningful learning to happen or not happen, it's the teacher who makes the difference.

When considering attitude and atmosphere, address these questions:

1) What specific things do I say and do to help my students know that they are valuable persons to me?
2) What are the pre-conditions which exist that could interfere with or inhibit my students' motivation and ability to learn?
3) Do I expect my students to show respect for me by first modeling my respect for them?
4) In what ways do I encourage my students to want to "buy into" what I am teaching?
5) What kinds of situations do I set up as challenges to keep my students motivated to learn?
6) Are my students free to take learning risks during the music lesson? Do they respond without fear of failure?
7) What kinds of responses do I see and hear from my students that indicate that meaningful learning is going on?
8) What kinds of positive reinforcers do I use to nurture student participation?
9) Prioritize these objectives: Motivate students to want to learn. Teach students how to think. Teach content material.
10) If I were a student in my own music class, would I find the experience stimulating, boring, intriguing, meaningless, challenging, fun, intimidating or exciting? Why or why not?

E F F E C T I V E
MUSIC TEACHING

Based upon 17 years of music teaching experience, and collaboration with numerous master teachers, it is suggested that music teaching is effective teaching when these conditions are met:

- A child's self-esteem is addressed.
- A child is made aware of course content and learning expectations (learning outcomes are the result of the actual teaching/learning experience).
- A child's learning readiness level, and individual learning style are accurately assessed, and included in researching, planning, preparing and delivering the music lesson.
- The top priority for a child in each music lesson is not WHAT to learn but HOW to learn.
- A child's curiosity is aroused, and attention is captivated through the use of varied motivational techniques.
- A child's use of critical-thinking skills and decision-making skills is continually encouraged.
- A child's effort is continually encouraged.
- A child's improvement and growth in the acquisition of musical concepts and skills, and other learning behaviors, is accurately assessed.

Meaningful learning is an on-going process that thrives in a non-judgmental, non-threatening climate of unconditional acceptance and encouragement. Following are some suggestions for developing a positive teaching attitude and an atmosphere of unconditional acceptance and encouragement. These guidelines can help trademark your music lessons as "success experiences" for children.

HEALTHY
SELF CONCEPT

PHILOSOPHICALLY SPEAKING

Consider building each lesson plan from this premise: The fact that children can make beautiful music is less significant than the fact that music can make beautiful children.

SOUL FOOD

It is recognized that the quality of a child's self-concept is a significant factor in predicting his/her learning success in school. A healthy self-concept is a pre-requisite for attending, concentrating and retaining. Children reach their greatest learning potential when they feel good about themselves, and a child's self-concept can be continually nourished by the music teacher. Find ways to show your students that they are precious to you, and held in your highest regard. For instance:

> **"The fact that children can make beautiful music is less significant than the fact that music can make beautiful children."**

"Eric, I'm really glad that you're my music student again this year. I guess I'm really a lucky teacher."

"Brandon, it's kids like you who make me glad I'm a teacher."

"Krista, even though it appears that you're the student and I'm the teacher, I always learn a lot of things from YOU. Thank you for sharing yourself with me."

WINNERS AT LEARNING

Children may not automatically view themselves as capable learners in the music room. Reaffirm your belief in them that they are capable of not only meeting tremendous learning challenges, but also achieving mastery of many musical skills. Remind them that they possess their own "personal power" to be "winners at learning." This attitude is contagious. A child's ability to learn and perform is directly related to the teacher's belief that he/she can. Children can learn to foster that belief in themselves, too.

"Kennedy, thank you for taking the time to THINK. I can't wait to see how you're going the notate the end of your song."

"Jenna, it looks like you enjoy trying new things. I like your attitude, 'I can try.' You are truly a learning champion."

A MIRROR IMAGE

"The me I SEE is the me I'll BE." Recognize the strong points of each child, and remind him/her of those qualities as often as possible. Children mirror the image of themselves held by their teacher, and, with repeated nurturing, they can learn to see themselves in their best light.

CELEBRATE LEARNING

Consider this thought: Each day is a new chance to celebrate our children's individual learning potential through music. Find many and different ways to make sure students know this.

"Alyssa, I admire your ability to remember rhythms exactly the way you hear them. You're fortunate to have a good memory."

"Kristine, you sure seem to enjoy singing. Would you like to lead the next song?"

"Nicholas, that is really a great question. Before I offer my idea of an answer, what do YOU think?"

PROCESS VS. PRODUCT

> **"The me I SEE is the me I'll BE."**

The learning process is more important than the musical product, except for a performance. Stress to children that, within the music class, it's not perfection that a music teacher expects and evaluates, but rather, improvement and growth in learning.

COLLABORATION VS. COMPETITION

Throughout this book, emphasis is placed on collaboration among children, not competition. Competition produces a winner and a loser, and a loser's only gain is a damaged self-concept. Competition also tends to foster a boastful attitude in children which says: "I must out-do whatever you can do." Collaboration, however, exemplifies an attitude which serves to build or restore self-concept: "Whatever you and I can do alone might be even greater if we do it together." With collaboration, every child is a winner.

THE PRIDE POSTER

The PRIDE poster is a sign which can be made and placed outside or inside the music room. It can be lettered this way:

pride (prīd) *noun.* The feeling a person has of his/her own worth and importance; self-respect. Although he was very poor, Mozart never lost *pride* in his musical accomplishments.

MUSIC AND ME

At the start of the school year, give all upper-elementary music students a piece of paper. Have them jot down the one thing they like best about music, and the one thing they like best about themselves, that they'd like you, their teacher, to remember about them. Be sure to include student's name (only for your recollection). Collect the papers. Treat the class to a self-concept review of their own group of "Stellar Citizens" by sharing these positive self-revelations without mentioning the names (for confidentiality).

THE BEST ME IS THE ONE YOU SEE

For younger children, hold a mirror as they enter the music room. Ask each child to see him/herself in the mirror. Invite each one to say the thing they like best about themselves. Highlight the comment by repeating it for all to hear. Make sure to look in the mirror and mention your favorite quality, too. (It might be something other than a physical attribute. Children can be led to realize that many personal strengths are qualities that can't be seen with the eyes, but can be "seen with the heart.") During the lesson, sing a song about positive self-esteem, or one that highlights the uniqueness of every individual.

> "Children can be led to realize that many personal strengths are qualities that can't be seen with the eyes, but can be 'seen with the heart.'"

MISSED YOU

If students are late, or if the classroom teacher inadvertently forgets about music class, consider getting the children yourself. This action tells students that they are far too valuable for you to forget. Greet them with: "The music room was so dull without YOU there! I MISSED you!" March them down the hallway with a rhythmic chant. Children love the attention from onlookers who happen to be in the hallway, and you are observed doing a fun and creative hallway maneuver.

NICKNAMES

Allow each music group to choose its own musical nickname. Here's an example: Mr. Smythe's Songsters, Mrs. Wilson's Warblers, or Ms. Aeplers's Arpeggios. During cooperative-learning group experiences, it's more fun play on a team with a name. Nicknames also lend a unique identity to the group as well as boost the spirit of fun and camaraderie for everyone in the class.

IT'S MY TURN

• Encourage students to whisper the answer to a question in your ear. This way, many children get a chance to answer the same question. Use facial expressions which show excitement, surprise, humor, pride, etc. Young children and grown-ups bond more quickly with "secrets" and other little shared intimacies. It may take a few extra moments of time, but the lucky teacher knows that children who feel treasured now, are secure, motivated learners later.

• Another similar tactic which encourages individual responses is to pose a question and ask students to put a finger on the nose, or fold the arms when they've thought of an answer. You can look about the class and positively note "who's thinking."

FLEETING THOUGHTS

If a student raises his/her hand to respond and forgets what to say, feelings of embarrassment are likely. An attitude of acceptance can "save face" for this person. A comment such as:

"Oh, Lindsey, that happens. Not to worry. Keep thinking and the idea will pop back into your mind."

MODEL PERFORMERS

Students with observable patterns of inappropriate behavior suggestive of a poor self-concept can be selected as "models" when highlighting specific, musical skills. For instance:

"I notice that Courtney tightly covers her recorder holes. Won't she be glad when she hears herself play a nice, clear tone?"

"Chuck's manuscript is particularly clear and precise. I'll always be able to read his musical message."

PEER POWER

Note a student whose lack of a healthy self-concept inhibits him/her from being a learning participant. Choose this individual to help you demonstrate a new skill or technique. By deliberately selecting a student with the greatest need for attention, and placing him/her in a position of peer power and responsibility, the self-concept is nourished.

"Watch how Jeff and I play the scale together on the bells. Now, see if you can do it just like he did. Jeff, thank you for helping me teach."

CAUTION: LEARNING NOISE

One of the characteristics of a music room where success thrives is the evidence of "learning noise." This should not be a threat to music teachers, parents or administrators. In a music room, it's O.K. to hear meaningful learning going on. This type of music room is hallmarked by friendliness, spontaneity, joviality, equality and sharing.

> **"By deliberately selecting a student with the greatest need for attention, and placing him/her in a position of peer power and responsibility, the self-concept is nourished."**

POSITIVE REINFORCERS

WELL-DESERVED

Give stickers, stamps or awards to students for immediate positive reinforcement. Other awards can be favorite jobs, roles, etc. such as playing a beloved instrument, leading a song, or being a team captain. Use the awards in Chapter 12, or adapt.

Note: Although the concept of *achievement as its own reward* is a noble one, it is a lofty one for the student who has not often experienced the thrill of achievement. This student lacks the internal drive to even desire to achieve. External motivators, such as stickers, stamps, prizes, awards and other incentives whet the learning appetite. Each time a student experiences self-satisfaction (internal reward) from having achieved a personal goal or success, the need for incentives (external rewards) diminishes in both number and degree.

ENCOURAGEMENT VS. PRAISE

Freely use encouragement to reinforce a sincere effort. Encouragement is different from praise in that it focuses on, and highlights a specific behavior. Praise merely verbalizes the teacher's feelings. Hear the difference:

> ▶ **"Freely use encouragement to reinforce a sincere effort."**

"Jessica, that was great!" (praise)

"Jessica, I see that you were able to play the melody pattern on the bells with the correct rhythm." (encouragement)

APPLAUSE, PLEASE

Give applause for especially concerted efforts. Offer a robust "Bravo!" for immediate positive reinforcement; or, "Good! Shall we give that one another try?" for an honest assessment of an effort which invites improvement.

GOOD NEWS

Send home notes and/or photos of "noteworthy achievements," even if they only describe improved behavior or effort. Children love to receive their own mail, share the "good news" with a grown-up at home, and revel in the reminder of "a job well done," especially if it's posted on the refrigerator door, and later placed in a scrapbook with other meaningful mementos. See reproducible stationery in Chapter 12.

ONE OF A KIND

Invite children to create colorful drawings that show their favorite part of music. Post these outside the music room (like wallpaper), so that the pictures and messages are visible from the hallway. As they enter the music room, incoming groups of children see these drawings and messages, and are reminded of the joys of music-making, as pictured by their peers. Comment on the "wallpaper":

"The wallpaper is so unique and special - there isn't another school in the entire world with THIS wall! Thank you for creating a part of our very wonderful music wall!"

WORD POWER

FOREVER FRIENDS

• Address all students as "friends." When calling on one another, invite a student to "choose another friend."

• Freely speak the language which respects all children. For example:

"I notice... I care... I hope... I like... I appreciate... I'm glad... Please... Thank you... If you don't mind... I remember... Good for you... What do you think?... You're really trying hard... Hang in there!... Go for it...! Congratulations!... Give yourself a hand!"

When speaking to children, it helps to think of them as a teacher's best friends.

CONSIDER THIS AN INVITATION

When presenting an assignment, invite students into the activity, rather than commanding. For example:

"Let's consider..."
"Please give some thought to..."
"Why not try..."

A CLOSE SHAVE

When constructive criticism is due, it's safer to "lather someone up before shaving them." Make a positive comment, then follow it with constructive criticism.

"Briana, I noticed that you played all the correct bars for the xylophone accompaniment. Now, this time let's concentrate on making the rhythm more accurate."

THE EVOLVING FAMILY

When referring to a child's family, give some thought to the changing concept of "family." It is no longer appropriate to assume that a child comes from an environment where two adults, both of whom are the child's natural parents, live with the child. In conversation with a child, substitute the phrase "the grown-up who cares for you" for the word "parents." It is also inappropriate to assume that other children living in the same environment are siblings. Refer to them as "other children who live with you" instead of "brothers and sisters."

EYE TO EYE

Use "smiling eye contact" when giving or demonstrating instructions. With small children, be down at their level.

NEVER A WRONG ANSWER

ACCEPTANCE GUARANTEED

Dignify all earnest responses, correct or not. Even a well-thought-out, incorrect response deserves acknowledgment:

"John, I can tell that you're really thinking about that one."

"Elizabeth, how did you know the answer to my NEXT question! May I please ask the question in a different way?"

"Chad, that's our first idea. Let's brainstorm like Chad for some more ideas."

"Ramie, let's try your idea. If it works, great! If not, that's O.K., too. Maybe you can find a different way for the next time we do this activity."

A trusting relationship between student and teacher is nourished when a child's earnest ideas are unconditionally accepted. An unconditionally accepted child feels safe to learn in his/her own style and try new ideas without fear of rejection.

SELF-EVALUATION

As much as possible, keep the "group self-concept" intact. Damage to a few children's feelings can have a "domino effect" on others in the class. Group self-evaluation helps. For example: "You know what I expect. Now, what grade would YOU give yourselves for that latest effort?" Chances are, children being modest in their self-evaluations are further motivated to try harder to live up to their own expectations.

> "At all costs, avoid tactics which utilize humiliation, intimidation, and sarcasm when correcting a student."

NO HARD FEELINGS

At all costs, avoid tactics which utilize humiliation, intimidation, and sarcasm when correcting a student. Although grown-ups might appreciate the humor in this form of well-intentioned, constructive criticism, children seldom have the maturity and social experience which enable them to laugh at their own mistakes in the midst of their peers.

SPECIAL
TIMES

BIRTHDAYS SOUTH OF THE BORDER

Celebrate student birthdays which fall on music lesson days. The class sings *A Calypso Birthday Party* (song on page 12). The birthday child, seated at the place of honor (perhaps the piano bench), chooses a friend to draw a large cake, while he/she accompanies the beat of the song on a bongo drum. At the conclusion of the song, the birthday child taps the correct number of years on the drum, while the friend draws the same number of candles on the cake. The birthday child makes a wish, "blows out" the "candles," and the "flames" disappear with a whisk of the eraser. Applause.

GET-WELL WISHES

Why not entertain a student or staff member who becomes ill or hospitalized with a specially-created cassette tape of favorite songs, musical anecdotes and other fun and cheerful musical quips? Designate a class to perform for the recording, and a parent or other teacher to deliver the tape.

"A CALYPSO BIRTHDAY PARTY"

Cheryl Lavender

Lyrics (verse 1 / verse 2 / verse 3):

Hap-py Birth-day *Jas - on*, how— old are you? Will you tell the an - swer? Can you give a clue? You are grow-ing it's plain to see.

fun to grow— a lit-tle more each day? Are you glad we met— as friends a - long the way? You're as spec-ial as you can be. Play the Birth-day Bon - go for me!

close your eyes— and make a wish or two. And I hope that each— and ev-'ry dream comes true. Just be the best you can be.

It's a Ca-lyp-so Birth-day Par - ty!— It's a Ca-lyp-so Birth-day Par - ty!— It's a Ca-lyp-so Birth-day Par - ty! Play the Birth-day Bon - go for me!

Is it / Now me! Cha! Cha! Cha!

Accompaniment:

(Experiment with these rhythms, or improvise new ones.)

Drums:

Maracas:

Claves:

Guiros:

Cowbells:

Cabaca:

ALMA MATER

Positive school-esteem can be encouraged through the writing of a school song. Set a deadline for lyric suggestions. (Encourage students to write short phrases of words which best describe the many and different aspects of life at your school.) Upon collecting the lyric ideas, choose a public domain (not copyrighted) melody, and adapt new lyrics to fit, or create an entirely new melody. Rework as many of the phrases as possible, so that many are used. Reword as necessary to rhyme the ends of phrases. Pride is instilled in students and teachers alike by singing the "school's anthem" at the start of every assembly, sporting event, or concert.

TUNE-A-GRAMS

Present Tune-a-Grams (the official music room telegram) to school staff members, or visiting community members for special events such as birthdays, honors, retirements, donations, etc. For each occasion, designate a small group of student singers to sing *Happy Birthday* to the special grown-up (adapt new words to fit the occasion), and, present the Tune-a-Gram. See page 202.

THE SIXTH
SENSE

SELF-EFFACING HUMOR

Of all the senses, perhaps the most important sense at play in the music room should be the "sixth sense" - sense of humor! Laughter washes the soul, and renews an optimistic outlook. Self-effacing humor, a special technique utilized by the teacher can help children see their teacher as human, and endear one to the other. Once, when a music teacher was complimented by her students on her enormous singing range, she took a deep bow and said:

"Why, thank you. I've been told before that I have a big mouth!"

> **"Of all the senses, perhaps the most important sense at play in the music room should be the 'sixth sense' – a sense of humor!"**

STRESSING THE DOWNBEAT

A student inadvertently burps aloud in music class. Humoring the student takes away the embarrassment, and puts the control into the teacher's hands with a little comment:

"Scott, it wouldn't have been as noticeable if you would have done it on the beat."

IT'S JEST MUSIC

Timely little jokes or riddles can ease the daily tensions that become etched in your students' faces, or liven up a sluggish class. Even a groan or two, provides some comic relief at the right moment. Label these: "mind benders," "brain burners," "brain ticklers," "mind teasers," or simply announce, "It's music brain drain time!" Here are some favorite little gems that were shared by children:

What is the difference between a fish and a guitar?
You can't tuna fish.

Which pets are the most musical?
Trumpets.

Why are cows good musicians?
They make moo-sic.

First Boy: *My dad can play the piano by ear.*
Second Boy: *That's nothing! My dad can fiddle with his beard.*

What is a cat's favorite song?
Three Blind Mice.

What kind of automobile makes funny music?
A cartoon.

2 CLASSROOM MANAGEMENT AND DISCIPLINE

THE TEACHER / STUDENT RELATIONSHIP

The word "discipline" comes from the word "disciple." According to a dictionary definition, a disciple is one who accepts and assists spreading the doctrines of another. In other words, a teacher. A music teacher's discipline then, is really not a form of punishment that is done to children, but rather, an on-going approach, or method, that when conscientiously practiced with children over time, nurtures the kind of climate necessary for meaningful, musical learning to occur.

Meaningful teaching and learning do not always occur in ideal, or even favorable conditions, and factors which enter into the teaching/learning relationship are often unpredictable. For example:

- unsatisfactory classroom conditions
- lack of appropriate teaching materials
- class assignment overload
- unmanageable class size
- large percentage of learning-disruptive individuals in same class
- lack of networking support group
- students from neglectful or abusive environments
- wide cross-cultural and ethnic diversity of students
- students' lack of appropriate learning behaviors

And yet, throughout history, many fine teachers have taught well, and students have learned well, regardless of circumstances or other unpredictable factors. Since it is often impossible to arrange or control the conditions under which music teachers teach, or to specify the types of students music teachers might agree to teach, the secret of achieving a successful teaching/learning experience lies not outside, but inside the teacher/student relationship.

Sensitive music teachers invite shared thinking with students on the jobs that exist in the music room. And that's not just the student's job. Both teacher and student have co-existing jobs: to teach and to learn. Carrying out those jobs without interference or interruption demands a common system of principles under which both are governed. Together with music students, the sensitive and realistic music teacher acquires a means of:

1) Establishing course expectations.
2) Drawing up principles, guidelines or rules.
3) Indicating predicted outcomes, or consequences.

MUSIC CLASSROOM
MANAGEMENT

"On the first day of music class, establish principles, guidelines, or rules that help govern both teacher and students in their jobs."

1) On the first day of music class, define the roles of both teacher and student. Engage your students in a conversation:

"As a music TEACHER, my job is..."

"As a music teacher, one of my roles is to share my expectations with you. Some of the ways that I can be the best teacher I can be are..."

"Things that could get in the way of my teaching are.."

"As a music STUDENT, my job is..."

"Some of the ways in which I can best learn are..." *"Things that could get in the way of my learning are..."*

2) On the first day of music class, establish principles, guidelines, or rules that help govern both teacher and students in their jobs. Using the chalkboard or a large chart, list all guidelines/rules volunteered by the children. They will perceive that they have some control over this activity, and are more apt to follow the principles/guidelines/rules which they themselves draw up.

List the principles/guidelines/rules under five categories:

    a) Attitude
    b) Effort
    c) Responses
    d) Learning Space
    e) Feelings

For example, here is a set of principles developed by a fifth grade music class from questions generated by the music teacher, and posted in the music room:

MUSIC ROOM PRINCIPLES:
CHOOSING MY PERSONAL POWER FOR LEARNING

1) Choose a thinking attitude. Fill the mind with questions.

2) Choose learning behaviors that show the best possible effort. Say: "I can try my best."

3) Choose to take turns when sharing:
    • solutions to problems
    • answers to questions
    • new ideas

4) Choose to occupy own learning space in a manner which:
    • shows dignity and respect
    • is free of distractions that interfere with teaching or learning

5) Choose comments and actions which are positive, kind and constructive.

Most music classes establish principles/guidelines/rules fairly early in the school year. What happens AFTER this point determines the kind and quality of classroom management which hallmark the discipline practiced in your music room. Consider the following strategies when formulating or enhancing your own unique style of classroom management.

ACKNOWLEDGING
APPROPRIATE BEHAVIOR

ME, FIRST

Volunteer to be the first person in the music room to follow the principles. When a principle is modeled by the teacher and results in a successful outcome, it makes more sense to students that they might consider it, too. Occasionally, throughout the school year, invite your students to catch you in the act of following a music room principle, and present YOU with a sticker or other award. This tactic shifts the focus on "whose behavior is being observed," and gives students an opportunity to critique the music teacher. Also, catch yourself in the act of violating one of the principles, and mention it aloud to the group. Students learn to accept their teacher as a human being involved in the life-long process of learning, too.

MODEL BEHAVIOR

Encourage appropriate behavior by highlighting and rewarding individual, specific behaviors. For example:

"Students who demonstrate that they can complete their theory sheet while showing respect for others at their music table may select the instrument of their choice for rhythm band. Here are some ways of showing respect that I'll be observing:

- *Sharing group pencils and markers at the table.*
- *Helping a friend who needs assistance.*
- *Quietly putting all materials away in correct places."*

Stickers, stamps, music awards, or just the mentioning of children's names aloud can positively focus on the behaviors that model exemplary discipline. Be sure to highlight the appropriate behavior of a student who is frequently challenged to behave appropriately. This technique is a proven way to raise a student's sense of self.

THINKERS GALORE

Create a program within your music room that aims to positively reinforce the evidence of thinking skills. At the start of the school year, tell every group of music students that any time you catch any of them in the act of THINKING (responding to a question, attempting a new playing technique, thinking of a friend with helpful actions, asking a thought-provoking question, etc.) they could receive an award, such as a sticker, or a stamp on the back of the hand. Award thinking students randomly.

> ▶ "Tell every group of music students that any time you catch any of them in the act of THINKING, they could receive an award."

Before any student can receive a second sticker, every student in the class must have received one first. Keep track in the gradebook. From that time on, each student is invited to receive as many additional rewards as you desire to offer. After the first award, it is no longer necessary to keep track. By waiting until each member of your music class has contributed something to the group's cumulative act of thinking, you are underscoring your belief that each and every student can think and learn, and that these abilities are of great value to you, their teacher.

CAUGHT IN THE ACT

Whenever possible, send a note home, or to the classroom teacher which describes a student who got caught in the act of thinking. A very brief description of the behavior verifies the earnest effort in the minds and hearts of other adults, who also feed into that student's self-concept.

WHOLE-GROUP BEHAVIOR MANAGEMENT

• Establish a "music shop." Ahead of time, cut out dozens of paper note heads, for use as tokens. (Parent helpers or student helpers are often available for this kind of service.) Paper notes can be given by the teacher to a student who demonstrates any number of exemplary behaviors. For example, tokens can be given for: music assignments, extra credit bonus points, suggestions, new ideas, appropriate conduct, and more. Create a "cash register" from a cardboard box. Determine the number of tokens which can be cashed in for selected awards.

Awards can be certificates, ribbons, stickers, stamps, more tokens, or a raised music grade. The incentives are as varied as the teacher who creates the music shop. When a student receives a token note, his/her name is printed on the back, (with a pencil conveniently attached to the cash register) and saved in the cash register. Quarter, term or semester conclusions are good times for cashing in the tokens. A whole-group reward (such as a popcorn party, the playing of a favorite recording or video, a musical "choice" day, etc.) can be given to an entire group of music students who accumulates a predetermined number of points eligible for the reward.

• Here's a whole-group, behavior management program which daily monitors students' behavioral progress with the aid of a visual chart. Create a large chart showing a treble music staff, as shown (this chart shows a goal of 25 points, however, the goal for your individualized music program may require more or less points):

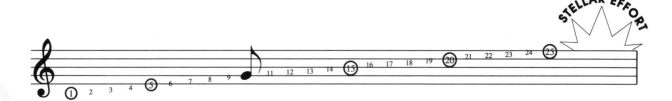

Cut out an appropriately-sized eighth note. Number each line of the staff in the manner shown. With very small lines, also indicate the numbers between the lines. The object of this program is for students to move the eighth note up the staff to the "Stellar Effort" place. Students do this by demonstrating appropriate behavior during music class. The Rule: The music note may move only up, and it never moves down. Encourage students to use thinking statements/behavior to advance their music note up the staff. A total of five points may be earned during one music class, one point for each of these demonstrated behaviors:

1) Students find places in an efficient manner.
2) Song books, papers, instruments and other supplies are handled appropriately.
3) Words which give dignity and respect are heard.
4) Courtesy is shown for another's learning space.
5) Line-up is accomplished in an acceptable manner.

At the end of the music lesson, the teacher and students share a mini-conference to decide the total number of points earned for that lesson. A student may be chosen to secure the note to the proper place on the music staff. When the music note reaches 25 points, (or the number of points deemed necessary to establish a pattern of appropriate group behavior), the whole class earns the "Stellar Effort" award, also posted on the staff chart. The grand prize can be stickers, stamps, the playing of a favorite recording or video, a musical "choice" day, a popcorn party, and more. When a "Stellar Effort" is achieved, the program can begin again.

Note: When a student, because of repeated inappropriate behaviors, single-handedly keeps the group from advancing the music note, he/she requires additional behavior management. Please note following section, "Dealing with Inappropriate Behavior - the C.Y.B. Program." If this individual receives three C.Y.B. assignments during the designated time period, he/she is excluded from the group grand prize.

STICKER ART

For teachers who utilize individual student folders which contain music sheets, songs, and more, place stickers and/or stamps as rewards for appropriate behavior, homework assignments, extra credit bonus points, etc. right on the front or inside cover of the student's folder. At the end of a designated time period, the total number of stickers/stamps is tallied for pre-determined awards.

▶ "When a student single-handedly keeps the group from advancing the music note, he/she requires additional behavior management."

MOST IMPROVED BEHAVIOR

The "Most Improved Behavior" reward for a very young student can be a turn with the music teacher to:

1) Play the piano - teacher plays a round or canon, while student plays the "sol" pitch (5th scale degree) one octave higher with a steady beat, in the treble (like a one-note descant).
2) Play the guitar - while seated, teacher holds guitar in the usual way, and fingers chords, while student stands behind and reaches over the body of the guitar to strum the strings with a steady beat.
3) Play the autoharp - while seated, teacher holds autoharp in the regular way and pushes chord bars, while student strums the strings.

DEALING WITH
INAPPROPRIATE BEHAVIOR

THE C.Y.B. PROGRAM

When a student violates a music room principle, and the teacher is compelled to intervene, some steps can be taken which focus on the consequences of the behavior while leaving student self-concept intact. The C.Y.B. program is a disciplinary, teaching tool which gives a student control over his/her own behavior by offering opportunities within the music class to self-correct inappropriate behavior. If a student is unable to self-correct inappropriate conduct, the teacher provides learning consequences.

1) In advance, the music teacher explains the natural consequences which occur when teaching or learning is interrupted - both teacher and students are unable to do their jobs. A reminder, known as a C.Y.B. (Check Your Behavior) is earned by (not given to) a student who violates a music room principle. The teacher acknowledges the infraction by calmly saying, "Sherrine, C.Y.B.," and continues to teach. If necessary, the teacher can whisper in the student's ear which music room principle is being violated. The student who earns the C.Y.B. is in charge of his/her own behavior, and has just been reminded in a tactful, dignified manner by the teacher, to check it.

2) For a second violation, the teacher repeats, "C.Y.B." The student is again reminded to correct his/her own behavior. For a third violation during the same music class, a third "C.Y.B." is earned, and if necessary, an alternate location for the student is found. A respectable title for the alternate location within the music room is: the "Time Away" place, rather than the "Time Out" place. The student is accompanied to the "Time Away" place with these words:

"Sherrine, you are welcome back to the music lesson, when you can bring the Sherrine who can follow our classroom principles. Let me know when she's ready to come back."

If finding an alternate location is impractical, the teacher quietly reminds the student about staying after class for a mini-conference. The music lesson resumes.

3) At the end of the music lesson, the mini-conference is shared by teacher and student for three purposes:

a) To offer empathy to the student for having earned three C.Y.B.'s.

b) To offer the student an opportunity to recall the three behaviors for which he/she received the three C.Y.B.'s.

c) To offer the student an opportunity to describe three appropriate behaviors which he/she can choose for the following music class, to replace the three inappropriate behaviors. If desired, the teacher can jot down the three choice behaviors right into the lesson plan book, and have the student initial it. This action gives the student some control while it bonds both teacher and student together in a united, disciplinary effort.

Note: Steps four through nine apply only to a student capable of completing a music assignment on paper (typically grade 2 and older).

4) The teacher reminds the student to bring a pencil and paper to the following music class. The student is to "make up" the part of the lesson (on paper) which he/she was unable to complete during the current music class, due to learning time spent in the "Time Away" area, or lost through inappropriate behavior.

> **"During the following music class, the student is seated apart from the rest of the group, and is otherwise able to hear or see the music lesson."**

5) During the following music class, the student is seated apart from the rest of the group, (perhaps in an area of the classroom designated as "the Productive Thinking Space," or, the "Time Away Place") and is otherwise able to hear or see the music lesson. It is here that he/she completes a prepared music assignment from the previous lesson (a theory page or music activity sheet which correlates with current unit of music study).

Any portion of the prepared music assignment which is not completed during this music lesson is to be completed at home or on recess, signed by a parent/guardian, and is due the following music lesson. The teacher:

a) Signs the assignment, with the school's telephone number.
b) Indicates the due date on the assignment (the date of the following music lesson).
c) Indicates a place on the assignment for the parent/guardian's signature.

6) Later, a phone call should be made to a parent/guardian at the student's home is in order to describe:

a) The behaviors which earned the three C.Y.B's.
b) The music lesson that the student is being required to complete on paper.
c) The way in which the parent/guardian can support (signing the music assignment). If an adult from home is unavailable, the principal is consulted for support. He/she signs the completed music assignment.

> **"It is helpful to remember that parents send to school the best children they have."**

Note: It is helpful to remember that parents send to school the best children they have. They may be having difficulty with their children at home, too, and, providing empathy can open the door to reciprocal, non-threatening communication.

7) When the assignment, signed by a parent/guardian from home, or principal, is submitted at the following music class, it becomes the "ticket for re-entry" into the music class.

8) When the music student gains entrance back into music class, teacher and student shake hands, and both begin a fresh, new slate. The teacher offers additional empathy:

"You know, Katie, I really like you, and I'm glad that you're my music student. And yet, I was unable to accept the behavior that you chose. Welcome back to class. I'm confident that you can bring the best Katie to our music lesson today. How does this make you feel?"

9) If the written assignment is not returned at the next music lesson, another page is assigned, and the student continues to participate from the "Time Away" place. If two such assignments are not completed or signed, a phone conference is scheduled with the parent/guardian, and together, a recommendation is made in the best interests of the student (perhaps an in-school conference with the principal) for future action regarding the student's musical learning progress.

Note: C.Y.B.'s are not "stockpiled" and accumulated from lesson to lesson. It is explained to students that mistakes happen to all people, and anyone can forget a guideline, or inadvertently break a rule. And, when music class is over, so are the C.Y.B.'s for that day. Each new day is a fresh, new start "to be the best that we can be."

> **"Each new day is a fresh, new start 'to be the best that we can be.'"**

THE
MUSI-CONTRACT

Occasionally, it becomes necessary to deal with an aggressively disruptive learner in an equally assertive manner. When a student holds the record of "repeat offender" (accumulating three C.Y.B.'s on several occasions), this individual requires a consistent program of on-task reinforcement, alternating with suspension from music class. The MUSI-CONTRACT is a disciplinary, teaching tool which:

• Secures an agreement between the learning-disruptive student and several adults (one of whom is the parent/guardian) and dictates the conditions under which the student may attend music class. The student is contractually bound to participate in music class ONLY by earning his/her attendance. Behavior in the music room is closely monitored, alternating with suspension in a supervised, alternate location.

• Offers the music teacher an improved teaching/learning climate by temporarily removing the inappropriate behavior from the music class.

• Teaches the learning-disruptive student a plan of earned rewards or consequences for choosing appropriate or inappropriate behavior. See MUSI-CONTRACT on page 27.

• Is both remedial and supportive in that the adults who enter into the contract agree to encourage the student to uphold the terms of the contract.

The MUSI-CONTRACT is implemented as follows:

1) The music teacher consults with the building principal before using the MUSI-CONTRACT, to provide update information regarding the learning-disruptive student's behavior problems. Typically, the principal has already acquired his/her own file of information regarding this individual's past record of behavior. When the principal is consulted in the initial stages of implementing the MUSI-CONTRACT, he/she is better equipped to comprehend and support the music teacher's actions.

2) The "alternate location" as specified in the MUSI-CONTRACT is recommended at this time, and is usually but not always, the principal's office.

3) The learning-disruptive student is invited to conference with the parent/guardian, music teacher, and classroom teacher in order to sign the MUSI-CONTRACT. If necessary, the principal is included for additional support. The conference date is established, and all invited persons are contacted. The conference is conducted in this manner:

a) A description of the problem is presented (inappropriate behaviors in the music room).

b) A description of interventions and all other tactics that have been tried as solutions, is presented.

c) The new plan, the MUSI-CONTRACT is explained. The terms of the contract are read by the student (if old enough), or by the music teacher.

d) Thoughts are shared on the terms of the contract in order to avoid any mis-communication. Everyone present must fully agree to the terms. Copies of the contract are then signed and dated by all present. Copies are distributed.

e) After a predetermined amount of time (for example, one month), a follow-up conference is arranged to evaluate the effectiveness of the MUSI-CONTRACT, and to make future recommendations as necessary.

4) If desired, the music teacher may include an incentive to help motivate the learning-disruptive student to achieve attendance for an entire music lesson. A "grab" into the "music grab bag" (a bag filled with inexpensive items such as musical pencils, erasers, pencil sharpeners, paper clips, kazoos, bookmarks and more - these can be purchased from the "boutique" department of most music stores) serves as an external reward for achieving attendance for an entire music lesson.

A) MUSIC ROOM PRINCIPLES:
CHOOSING MY PERSONAL POWER FOR LEARNING

1) Choose a thinking attitude. Fill the mind with questions.
2) Choose learning behaviors that show the best possible effort. Say: "I can try my best."
3) Choose to take turns when sharing:
- Solutions to problems
- Answers to questions
- New ideas
4) Choose to keep own learning space in a manner which:
- Shows dignity and respect
- Is free of distractions which interfere with teaching or learning
5) Choose comments and actions which are positive, kind and constructive.

B) THE CONSEQUENCE

1) If _____ chooses to violate a Music Room Principle,
Music Student

_____ assigns a C.Y.B. (Check Your Behavior).
Music Teacher

2) If three C.Y.B.'s are earned during a music lesson,_____ is immediately
Music Student

dismissed to:_____.
Alternate Location

_____ Number of minutes during which appropriate behavior was maintained.
_____ Time of dismissal from music class.

C) THE REWARD

1) _____ earns attendance in the following music class for the exact
Music Student

amount of time during which appropriate behavior was maintained in the previous music class.
The balance of time is to be spent in: _____.
Alternate Location

2) If _____ maintains appropriate behavior in the following music class
Music Student

for the designated amount of time, attendance during the next music class is to be extended by five
minutes, with the balance of time to be spent in: _____
Alternate Location

3) Attendance in subsequent music classes is to be extended by five-minute segments, or until an
entire music lesson of appropriate behavior is achieved.

_____   _____
Music Student   Classroom Teacher

_____   _____
Music Teacher   Parent

_____   _____
Principal   Date

MUSI-CONTRACT

SIMPLE BEHAVIOR
INTERVENTIONS

SECRET SIGNAL

Sometimes out of nervous habit, a student engages in gestures which inadvertently distract teaching and learning, for example: clicking a pencil, twirling long strands of hair around finger or pencil, wriggling about in the chair or desk, making mouth or throat sounds, manipulating coins or trinkets found in the pockets, and others. The student does not wish to purposely distract, and is often unaware that he/she is even doing so. This student is surprised, humiliated and offended when the behavior is treated as a "misbehavior."

Meet privately with this individual, and mention that the behavior interferes with teaching and learning. Together, brainstorm ideas for a signal from you which could catch the child's attention (without alerting others), and allow him/her to self-correct the behavior.

SMALL TALK

When talking or "chit-chatting" erupts while you're teaching, simply comment in an even-toned voice:

"Danny, I'll wait to continue, when I'm sure that everyone in the class can hear me. Thank you."

And then wait for silence.

HOT FINGERS

For a young student who is unable to refrain from playing a rhythm instrument until the appropriate time, suggest:

"Rebecca, will you please talk to your hands. Tell them only to play when I give the signal, O.K.? If your hands don't listen to you, then they will have to place the instrument back in its case, and the instrument will be sad, because it loves to sing."

A WRONG TURN

When students talk during another's turn, stop the turn and speak directly to the student:

"Emily, I know it's your turn to speak, but, someone else is taking your turn. Would you mind waiting to speak when that individual gives your turn back? Thanks."

SOLVING PROBLEMS

• When two or more students are involved in a dispute over materials, instruments, taking turns, etc. that does not appear easily solved, bring out the "solution table." The solution table serves as a "common ground" where students gather together to reach a solution to their problem. Have the students sit around the solution table, place the object of dispute on it (perhaps a favorite instrument), and allow a time-limit for brain-storming. If a mutually satisfactory solution is not reached within the time limit, the teacher chooses the course of action. When students are allowed to solve their own problems, they learn the fine art of negotiating as well as unlearn their dependence on the teacher to work out problems which belong to them.

> ▶ **"When students are allowed to solve their own problems, they learn the fine art of negotiating as well as unlearn their dependence on the teacher to work out problems which belong to them."**

• "The Peace Bond" is another way for students to solve their own problems. It is a piece of wide, cloth ribbon, approximately three feet in length, sewn together at both ends. (Musical motifs may be sewed or painted on the ribbon.) Have the students sit in a circle with the Peace Bond inside. All hands hold onto the Peace Bond until a mutual solution is reached.

3 INCREDIBLY SUCCESSFUL
TEACHING STRATEGIES

GENERAL TEACHING STRATEGIES

"If I don't have the time to teach it right, how will I ever find the time to teach it over?"

It's the challenge of every elementary school music teacher, stressed with too little time – to find teaching strategies that get the job done right without wasted time! The premise of this chapter is that by taking time to judiciously select teaching strategies now, precious class time is saved, later. Carefully prepared learning challenges can be thought-provoking, and odds are increased that children can become better learners every time they are strategically aroused into a thinking state. The following teaching strategies in Chapter 3 and Chapter 4 are presented to hopefully tickle your imagination (and your student's!) and propel you toward other creative ways of teaching.

THINKING ABOUT LEARNING
AND LEARNING ABOUT THINKING

THE LEARNING PROCESS

One of the most helpful thinking strategies is the adoption of this long-range view of the learning process:

1) A child must be exposed to a new concept by first experiencing it many times at the "unconscious" level.

2) Later, the concept is formally introduced, and made "conscious," by highlighting, analyzing, and transferring it to other experiences. The concept becomes meaningful.

3) Over time, the meaning of a new musical concept becomes internalized through repeated, related learning experiences.

For example, the concept of "verse/refrain" is first experienced many times through the actual singing of songs which have that form. The child participates in the experience of "verse/refrain," but is "unconscious," or, not cognizant of the meaning of "verse/refrain." Later, after a foundation of many song experiences is laid, the concept is then brought to a "conscious" level when it is formally introduced through the use of teaching techniques that highlight and analyze it. The concept becomes meaningful when the stored-up information about "verse/refrain" is transferred to other songs, and the child is challenged to:

a) Use critical thinking skills to synthesize into a "whole" all previously stored bits of information or "parts" about "verse/refrain."
b) Draw his/her own conclusions as to the concept's meaning and function.
c) Recognize and identify the form "verse/refrain" in other songs.

OUTCOME-BASED LEARNING

Children need to understand "where they have been, where they are presently, and where they are headed" in terms of their musical learning growth span. It has been recognized that children perform better at tasks when they know ahead of time precisely what is expected of them. Gathering information about your students equips you to:

• Teach from realistic objectives.

• Choose the most efficient teaching strategies.

You can raise the odds of your music students' successful learning outcomes by:

1) Evaluating your students' learning readiness by acquiring information about their prior musical learning experiences.
2) Becoming acquainted with your students' individual learning styles.
3) Informing your students of the expectations for each marking period. Describe the content of the final evaluation (test or the equivalent), as well as course content and projects.

> ▶ "Children need to understand where they have been, where they are presently, and where they are headed in terms of their musical learning growth span."

POWER THOUGHTS
Two thinking strategies that produce winning thinkers:

1) Tell children WHAT to do (solve musical problems) and let them figure out HOW to do it (brainstorm solutions for learning).
2) Instead of explaining a concept to children, set up a learning situation, then ask critical questions to help generate their thinking processes.

THE MUSIC
LESSON

THE LESSON PLAN/PREPARATION
Experiment with lesson plans which use this generic formula: (See sample Lesson Plan/Preparation on page 34.)

1) OPENER/REVIEW — describes the strategy for:
   a) welcoming everyone to the music lesson
   b) creating the learning climate
   c) encouraging a whole-group response with a known (or new) song or musical activity which includes a learned (old) concept(s)/skill(s)

2) NEW MATERIAL — describes the strategy for:
   a) exposing and/or introducing a new musical concept(s)/skill(s)
   b) highlighting or stressing a new musical concept(s), using one, two or more "teaching assistants" (students) as demonstrators

3) PRACTICE — describes the strategy for:
   a) transferring newly-learned concepts to songs, games, activities and skills which reinforce those concepts through critical thinking, moving, listening, reading, writing, singing, playing, interpreting, memorizing or creating
   b) practicing skills that stress learned (old) concepts from previous lessons
   c) encouraging individual and/or whole-group responses

4) CLOSURE — describes the strategy for:
   a) bringing the lesson to an end
   b) encouraging a whole-group response with a known song or musical activity
   c) assessing individual and/or whole-group musical learning outcomes

Grade: _____ Week Of: _____

Music Educator: _____

	LESSON 1	LESSON 2
SET-UP (materials)		
CONCEPT(S)		
OPENER/REVIEW Strategy for opening music lesson and reviewing concept(s)/skill(s)		
NEW Strategy for exposing/introducing new concept(s)/skill(s)		
PRACTICE Strategy for stressing/transferring concept(s)/skill(s)		
CLOSURE Strategy for assessing learning outcomes and closing the music lesson		
EXTENDED ACTIVITIES		

MUSIC LESSON PLAN/PREPARATION

(This page may be photocopied.)

SAYING TOO MUCH

• Strive to keep instruction and "teacher talk" to a bare, yet effective, minimum. Whenever possible, substitute speaking with demonstrating. For an ear-opening experience, let a hidden tape recorder record a music lesson. Later, with a critical ear, listen and note the percentage of lesson time spent on "teacher talk" and the percentage of time spent on music-making. Does it appear that, after a certain point, "teacher talk" becomes superfluous and wastes valuable teaching time?

• When speaking with students, share thoughts that include more questions than statements:

"What do you hear?"
"What do you observe?"
"What would happen if...?"
"What do you think about that?"

THE CONCEPT CHART

At the beginning of each music lesson, have the "concept chart" within easy view. It can be a large poster, wipe-away chart, or, the chalkboard. Select a student to print the "concept(s) of the day" and/or accompanying musical terms and symbols. The music lesson teaches the rest. The "concept chart" is the first and last visual aid that students see during the music lesson.

WHOLE GROUP MOVEMENT

How to get the children to engage in a new, whole-group movement activity? Use the "add-on" teaching strategy which teaches the new skill to only one or two "teaching assistants" (students), while the remaining music students observe. With mastery of the skill, the "assistants" choose new students to whom they teach the skill. These students become the new "assistants," and so it goes, until the entire class is involved.

WHOLE GROUP INSTRUCTION

When introducing a particular skill to an entire music class, select one or two students to act as "demonstrators." These students perform the task according to your instructions, while being observed by the remaining students in the group. Children are usually eager to teach one another, and conversely, children are eager to learn what other children have learned.

PARTNERS TEACHING PARTNERS

Children learn more efficiently when as many senses as possible are stimulated. With a partner, a student engages in an interpersonal contact, focuses on directionality in movement, refines cooperative, synchronized responses and actions, practices skills which reinforce visual, aural and kinesthetic styles of learning, and more. When partners are selected, children are paired up by the teacher, or allowed to choose. If there is one child without a partner, that one pairs up with the teacher, or observes until the next activity, then is allowed first choice for a partner.

Children sometimes choose their best friends for their partners. The unfortunate result is often hurt and rejected feelings, as well as damaged self-concepts of children who are not chosen. The following strategy for changing partners emphasizes the concept that every child in the music classroom is equally important:

1) Partners form two concentric standing circles; one partner in the inside circle, the other partner in the outside circle. Partners face one another.

▶ **"The act of creating puts a student at the center of his/her own learning experience and provides an opportunity to synthesize all previously learned bits of information into a uniquely perceived whole."**

2) At your command, "Shift gears..." outside circle of students moves one step to the left, and faces the "new" partner. Students are encouraged to say "Hello and howeryadoin?" Continue with next activity.

PROJECT CREATE

• Wrap up each learning unit with a creative music project. The act of creating puts a student at the center of his/her own learning experience, and provides an opportunity to synthesize all previously learned bits of information into a uniquely perceived whole. The experience of music-making becomes highly personalized for students who, for example, create their own unique rhythm or melody compositions, or tone color experiments. Some ideas follow later in the next chapter, but your own imagination can dictate just the right short or long-term activity to correlate with your individualized, music program.

MY VERY OWN MUSIC BOOK

Assign a music folder (a manila, letter-sized folder is inexpensive) to each music student:

1) On the tab goes the student's name, class and grade.

2) One entire music lesson is devoted to the art design of the front cover. While listening to music, students create a musical illustration or design depicting the music.

3) Into the folder go the school year's accumulation of songs, "practice pages," creative assignments, music notes and staff page assignments, etc.

4) Throughout the year, the collected materials are used for monitoring and assessing student progress.

5) At the conclusion of the school year, students are presented with certificates of participation as the final entry into the folder.

6) The folder is stapled together and presented to each student as his/her very own "music book" to keep as a memento of that year's music class.

MUSIC LESSONS ON VIDEO

Give some thought to having some of your music lessons videotaped. In the event of your absence, or just for children's viewing pleasure in watching their friends on TV, have the video tape handy for ready viewing.

4 INCREDIBLY SUCCESSFUL TEACHING STRATEGIES

SPECIFIC TEACHING STRATEGIES

▶ STRATEGIES FOR TEACHING BEAT

THE BEATNIK

Children can visualize the concept of *beat* with this strategy:

1) Select one child to be the "beatnik" and walk about the room at any desired pace, so long as the movements are steady, and evenly-paced (like the sound of a ticking clock, or the blinker on a car, etc.)

2) While this child moves at his/her own pace, the remaining students emphasize the footsteps by clapping with each step. The regular, steady clapping is an aural accompaniment to the visual act of stepping the beat.

3) Experiment with different tempos, leading students to the conclusion that "beat is always steady," no matter whether the tempo is fast or slow.

WELL-BEATEN

Children moving to the beat of music are only as limited as their imaginations! Allow them to discover unique ways of moving to the beat such as: pound fist into opposite palm, two fingers tap opposite palm, hands "crash" in upward and downward strokes like cymbals, arms sway like elephant trunks, arms "rock a baby," and more. See how many more motions and sounds your students can invent.

MUSICAL TRAFFIC SIGNAL

Very young children are getting acquainted with the feeling of beat, or pulse in music. Make a simple "STOP-GO" sign from red and green construction paper:

1) Cut an octagon shape from both colors.

2) Print "GO" on the green; "STOP" on the red.

3) Insert a tongue depressor between both pieces, so that part of it protrudes from the bottom (for a handle), and glue all together.

4) Children listen to music with a beat, and pat their own "heartbeats" in tempo, while viewing the "GO" sign.

5) When the sign is flipped so that "STOP" is in view, the patting stops, and children just nod their heads to the beat. At the "GO" sign, the patting resumes.

TRANSFER THE BEAT

Continue the "heartbeat" activity with very young children by giving each child a page filled with heartbeats drawn horizontally across the page. While listening to music with a beat, children transfer the concept of patting their own hearts to patting the pictures of heartbeats from left to right across the page (in the same direction that music notes move). Heartbeats are drawn like this:

BEAT NOTATIONS

Conclude the "heartbeat" activity by transferring the concept of patting the heartbeat, to drawing the heartbeat. Using the same page of heartbeats from preceding activity and the same music, invite children to draw a vertical line straight down, through each pictured heartbeat, moving from left to right, each time they feel the beat of music. (The vertical line they are drawing is the "stem" of a future quarter note.) At a later date, the concept of *quarter note* ♩ = *one heartbeat* is introduced and made conscious. Note example:

S T R A T E G I E S   F O R
TEACHING RHYTHM

SWITCH GEARS
• Many music students, young and old alike, get confused with the difference in concepts between *beat* and *rhythm*. While singing a familiar song, invite students to pat the beat or pulse of a song on their legs. At your signal (perhaps a ring on the triangle), switch to the rhythm, then at the same signal, resume the patting beat, etc.

• Later, ask children to silently sing the same song, and clap out the rhythm of the words. Invite another student to accompany this activity with a drum beat. At your signal, stop the rhythmic clapping and hear only the steady drum beat. At same signal, resume rhythmic clapping, thus reinforcing the concept that the *rhythm* is the combination of the long and short sounds of the words, while the *beat* is the steady pulse.

RIGHT BEFORE YOUR VERY EYES!
At the start of this school year, review last year's rhythms with this memory strategy.

1) Notate eight known rhythm patterns on flash cards.
2) Set the cards on a ledge.
3) Clap any one of the rhythm patterns. Students echo-clap.
4) Students locate the card which shows the correctly notated rhythm. Turn the card over.
5) Repeat with remaining cards.
6) Now that they're no longer visible, see who can clap out the entire eight cards as they appeared in order on the ledge, from left to right.

ECHO CLAPS AND THEN SOME
• Invite students to echo-clap rhythms they hear performed on bells, recorder, bicycle horn, slide whistle, kazoo, and other fun, less predictable instruments.

Echo-clapping rhythm patterns can become monotonous, unless students are encouraged to frequently echo with different body sounds. For example, echo-claps can become leg pats, head pats, foot taps, tongue clicks, goose honks and more.

"Echo-clapping rhythm patterns can become monotonous, unless students are encouraged to frequently echo with different body sounds."

• Try this logical sequence, so that echo-clapping becomes progressively more challenging with each experience:

1) Echo body-percussion rhythms which fill a four-beat measure.
2) Echo silent-motion rhythms, such as touching the nose, swaying the arms, bobbing up and down, etc. which fill a four-beat measure.
3) Echo combinations of body-percussion and silent-motion rhythms which fill a four-beat measure, after four beats of rest (silence).
4) One-half of the music group echoes the other half, who echo the teacher's combinations of body-percussion and silent-motion rhythms which fill a four-beat measure.
5) Perform canon combinations of body-percussion rhythms and silent motion rhythms which fill a four-beat measure, exactly one measure later than the teacher. Both teacher and students are performing simultaneously, except that the students are always one measure behind, and finish one measure after the teacher.
6) Repeat step 5 but instead of a two-part canon, create a three-part canon.

• After students have learned to echo-clap rhythm patterns, have them identify "same" or "different." Tap out three rhythm patterns on a tone block or drum. Two of the rhythm patterns are tapped alike, and one tapped differently. Students echo-clap the rhythm patterns and attempt to identify the pattern which did not "match." Perform several examples, and at a later date, allow students to lead the activity.

ROCKIN' RHYTHMICIANS

Make or obtain an easy rhythm band chart. Instead of all instruments playing all the rhythms, designate certain rhythms to be played only by certain instruments. For instance, ♪♪ = played by maracas, jingle taps, tambourines; and ♩ = played by drums, claves, cymbals, woodsticks, and so on. Students learn ensemble playing, and need to be "on their toes" in order to play only at appropriate times. See *Rockin' Rhythms* on page 61.

RHYTHM MATCH CARDS

When very young children have learned the basic rhythm patterns: ♩ ♫

1) Print eight, easy-to-read word phrases from children's reading vocabulary on the chalkboard, or large chart. (Prior to this, notate only the rhythms of each word phrase on eight flash cards.) For example:

puppy dog   puppy dog

run   run   running fast

2) Set the flash cards on a ledge, and read one of the word phrases aloud, while clapping its rhythm.
3) Children echo, then immediately search for the flash card which shows the correctly notated rhythm.
4) Remove the flash card from the ledge, and cross out the word phrase.
5) Continue in this fashion, until all eight word phrases are matched to the corresponding rhythm cards.
6) Erase the word phrases, and show each flash card. Allow students to recall the word phrase which fit. (The same concept practiced in reverse.)

RHYTHM IN SHOES

Very young students who have learned these notes: ♩ ♫ can verbalize action words that sound a rhythm pattern made with combinations of these notes. For example:

walk   walk run- run walk

As they enter the music room, lead them in this repeated chant, while moving your feet *in rhythm*. Invite them to imitate you while listening to music. This rhythm pattern is walked again and again around the room, and quickly becomes internalized.

THEMATIC MOVEMENT

Once basic rhythm patterns are learned, select a musical recording whose theme sounds known rhythm patterns, such as *Symphony #94, First Movement*, by Joseph Haydn (Surprise Symphony). Arrange students in a standing circle, facing one direction. Invite them to step the rhythm of the theme each time they hear it. For example:

run run run run run run walk

run run run run run run walk

run run run run run run walk

run run run run walk   jump!

RHYTHMIC SPEECH

For rhythmic accompaniments played on rhythm, melody or harmony instruments, create a catchy little word phrase that a student can chant, which sounds the same rhythm pattern as the accompaniment. For example, while repeatedly chanting, "Happy Birthday Happy Birthday," the student successfully plays repeated eighth note patterns on the instrument. See *A Calypso Birthday Party* on page 12.

Hap -py Birth-day Hap-py Birth-day

TUMMY YUMMIES

Once basic rhythm patterns are learned, create "Tummy Yummies" by arranging favorite foods into rhythmic phrases and discovering the corresponding music notes. See how many more "tummy yummies" your students can come up with!

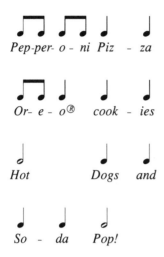

Pep-per- o - ni Piz - za

Or- e - o® cook - ies

Hot   Dogs   and

So - da   Pop!

Extend this rhythmic activity by substituting the names of people, places, colors, holidays and more.

MUSICAL NAMES

The rhythm of students' names can be notated, using combinations of these notes. For example, discover which students' names match this rhythm pattern. These names fit:

Da - vid   O - gil- vie

Mich - ael   Mac-In- tire

Cyn - di   Ja- cob-son

Find other names which correspond with other rhythm patterns. Students love discovering that they share a common musical element with peers. This is an easy and fun activity. Caution: be careful when notating the rhythm of names which sound on a "pick-up note," like:

E - liz- a -beth Stan - ley

La - Qui - sha   Wil - liams

An extension to this activity: Print all "like" names and corresponding notation on colorful cards, cut in the shape of music notes. The cards are strung in various lengths on a clothes hanger to which a colorful, tag-board music staff is attached. The end result is a musical mobile to hang in the children's regular classroom, or music room.

RHYTHM SLIDERS:

1) Glue two pieces of tag-board together at opposite ends, leaving the other two ends and middle open. This is the holder.

2) The slider is a narrower, but longer piece of tag-board.

3) Draw a series of rhythm patterns lengthwise, down the right half of the holder.

4) Cut out small "windows" on the left side of the holder, just in front of each rhythm pattern.

5) On the slider, draw newly-learned rhythm patterns that fit within the cut-out "windows" on the holder.

6) Draw the slider slowly through the holder and stop while students clap or play the rhythm patterns in view.

7) Allow students to lead the activity by operating the "rhythm slider" for classmates.

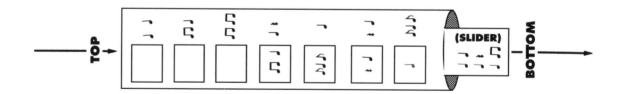

RHYTHM FLASH CARDS

Make or obtain a set of rhythm flash cards. Invite music students to clap or play instruments as you flash the cards, following this progressively challenging sequence:

1) Flash the cards, one at a time, with four beats of silence in between.
2) Flash the cards, one at a time, one right after another.
3) Flash the cards, one at a time, but have students clap the rhythm on the first card, *after* it has been flipped, when the second card is in view. Continue flashing the entire deck. This technique achieves the effect of "reading music in canon," and stimulates the development of music memory skills.
4) Ahead of time, designate certain rhythm patterns to be performed only by patting the legs, or clapping while popping up from the chairs, etc. The rest of the rhythms are to be clapped as usual while sitting down. For example:

$$\text{♩ ♩} = pat\ on\ legs \qquad \text{♪ ♩ ♪} = stand\ up$$

Note: When certain rhythm patterns are frequently misread, or incorrectly performed, remove those flash cards from the deck and put them in the "dog house" (the chalkboard ledge, or top of the piano). After the entire deck as been flashed, bring the flash cards out from the "dog house," and reinforce learning of those rhythm patterns before shuffling them back into the deck.

Just about the time your students think they are "pros" at these flash card techniques, allow them to flash the cards for one another.

FORWARD AND REVERSE

• When children are engaged in sight-reading rhythms, add some zip by challenging one-half of the music group to perform the rhythms forward, while the other half performs the rhythms in reverse.

• For advanced challenge, invite students to perform rhythms with the right hand patting the right leg, while the left hand canons the right hand, one measure behind on the left leg. You can really "smell the wood burning" in students' brains with this strategy!

AMBIDEXTROUS RHYTHMS

For an individual or cooperative project, have students create a fairly simple, four-measure rhythm at the chalkboard or a large chart. Have them decide which notes should be tapped out with the right or left hand. Right-hand notes are indicated with upward stems; left-hand notes, with downward stems. The rhythm may be tapped on a desk-top, or on the legs. When the rhythm is accurately performed, tell students to draw a repeat sign at the end of the fourth measure. The music is now an accompaniment, or "ostinato" to a favorite song. Sing a favorite song with the new body-rhythm accompaniment. See example:

Right Hand

Left Hand

RHYTHM DOMINOES:

1) Give each student a rectangular sheet of blank, heavy, oversized paper and marker, crayon or pencil.

2) Students draw a vertical line down the width of their "dominoes," showing two blank spaces.

3) Students fill up each blank square with one measure of rhythm in a specified meter.

4) Collect and scramble all dominoes.

5) Divide group into two cooperative-learning groups.

6) Designate a time limit, and using a stopwatch, time both groups as they build domino patterns using as many dominoes as possible.

7) When "time" is called, the team with the most used dominoes earns that exact number of points. For example, if a group successfully used seven dominoes, the group earns seven points.

8) Collect and scramble all dominoes.

9) Begin a second round, and play in the same fashion. Repeat as many times as desired.

Having designated a pre-determined number of points to win a group grand prize, total the cumulative points earned by both groups, and determine eligibility for the prize, which might be stickers, hand stamps, a favorite recording or song, a favorite video, recording or music game, etc.

Domino patterns are built as illustrated:

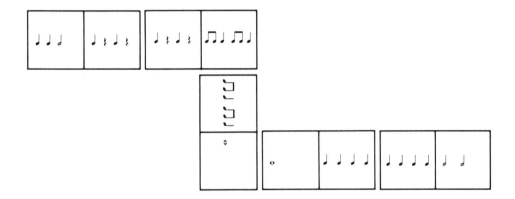

RHYTHM TELEPHONE

1) Draw a simple, four-beat rhythm on a card and place it face down.
2) Six to eight students sit in a line, all facing one direction.
3) Gently, with the two "pointer "fingers of each hand, press the rhythm inaudibly, into the back of the last student in line.
4) This student repeats the motion to the student in front, and so on.
5) When the first student in line receives the rhythm, ask him/her to notate it on the blank side of the same card.
6) Flip the card over and compare – did the rhythm stay the same, or did it change on its way through the line of students?
7) Try it again, with a new line of students, and have a student draw the new rhythm.

RHYTHM MEMORY MEASURES

1) At chalkboard or a large chart, draw a 4, 8, 12 or 16 measure rhythm sequence in a selected meter.

2) Conduct students through a clapping performance of the rhythms.

3) Erase one measure of rhythm.

4) Conduct students through a clapping performance of the rhythms a second time, including the erased measure.

5) Erase another measure.

6) Again, students clap out the entire rhythm sequence, including the two erased measures.

7) Continue activity in same manner, until all measures are erased, and the rhythms are "inside the head." The measures are clapped from memory in only a few minutes' time.

SCRAMBLED EGGS

• Need a strategy to reinforce *rhythmic sequence?* Try this game:

1) Select five or six known songs. Notate the first four measures of rhythm from each song onto separate, color-coded flash cards (each song on four cards of the same color).

2) Scramble each set of color-coded cards.

3) Have music students sing the words while clapping the rhythm to the first four measures of the first song.

4) Set the cards on a ledge in scrambled order.

5) Students work collaboratively to sequence the cards into the correct order.

6) Repeat this activity with the remaining songs.

• At a later time, make another, identical set of the same rhythm flash cards, and:

1) Divide the music class into two collaborative learning groups.

2) Each group is given a set of scrambled cards to the same song.

3) Announce the song title for the cards in Round #1, and time students with a stopwatch as they sequence the cards into the correct order.

4) The team that correctly sequences the cards in the shortest amount of time earns points equal to the number of seconds it took to achieve.

5) Continue in this fashion with remaining sets of cards.

6) Prior to this activity, designate the number of points for whole-group grand prize, such as stickers for all, singing a favorite song, certificates, listening to a favorite recording, watching a favorite video, etc.

7) Tally the total number of points from each round, and determine eligibility for the group grand prize.

S T R A T E G I E S   F O R
TEACHING METER

METER JIVES

It is easier and more natural for children to feel, or experience the metric divisions in music before reading and interpreting actual time signatures. *Meter* means measure. Describe to children how the beats of music are measured into sets, each set beginning with a strong, accented beat (in conductor's terms: the downbeat) and followed by the weaker beats. Show meter with the aid of this visual illustration:

Listen to a recording of music with *meter in four* (four beats to a measure). Any march by John Phillip Sousa is an excellent choice. Children are arranged in a sitting circle. Lead children in this whole-group hand jive which reinforces the feel of *meter in four*, while all repeatedly chant aloud: *"One, two, three, four."* (This meter jive also works for *meter in two*.)

1) Children pat own legs on "beat one."
2) Children pat the left leg of neighbor on the right on "beat two."
3) Children pat own legs on "beat three."
4) Children pat the right leg of neighbor on the left on "beat four."
5) Continue this pattern throughout the duration of the recording.

Or, invite students to perform their own hand jive, individually, like this:

1) Slap own legs.
2) Clap own hands.
3) Snap fingers, both hands.
4) Clap own hands.
5) Repeat

For *meter in three*, use this whole-group hand jive. Any of the famous walzes by Johann Strauss are excellent choices, or a child's favorite, *The Waltz of the Flowers* from *The Nutcracker Suite*, by Peter Tchaikovsky. (Begin the jive after the harp introduction).

1) Children clap own hands on "beat one."
2) Children "backhand slap" the backs of adjacent children's hands on "beat two."
3) Repeat step #2 on "beat three."
4) Continue this pattern throughout the duration of the recording.

Here's an individual hand jive for *meter in three*:

1) Slap own legs.
2) Clap own hands.
3) Snap fingers, both hands.
4) Repeat.

Here's a whole-group hand jive for *meter in two*:

1) Children sit in circle. Clap own hands.
2) Children "backhand slap" the backs of adjacent children's hands on "beat two."
3) Repeat.

COLLABORATIVE METERS I

• Another meter strategy pairs children into partners. Partners sit facing one another. Upon hearing a recording of music in a specific meter, invite the partners to experience the meter together:

1) Partners first listen to the music to determine when the strong, accented pulses occur.
2) At a strong pulse or downbeat, children clap their own hands.
3) On the weaker beats, partners clap each other's hands together.
4) Partners chant while clapping: "ONE, two, three, ONE, two, three..."
5) Continue this pattern throughout the duration of the music.
6) Use many different examples of musical styles in a variety of meters for challenge and reinforcement.

• Following are more "partner jives" in 4/4, 3/4 and 6/8 meters. Be sure to encourage partners to chant the counting out loud.

Partner Jive in *four*.
   1) Slap own legs.
   2) Clap own hands.
   3) Partners clap each other's right hands together.
   4) Clap own hands.
   5) Partners clap each other's left hands together.
   6) Clap own hands.
   7) Partners clap both hands together.
   8) Clap own hands.
   9) Repeat.

Partner Jive in *four*.
   1) Partners clap each other's right hands together.
   2) Clap own hands.
   3) Partners clap each other's left hands together.
   4) Clap own hands.
   5) Partners clap both hands together.
   6) Clap own hands.
   7) Cross own arms and tap shoulders.
   8) Slap own legs.
   9) Repeat.

Partner Jive in *four*.
   1) Partners slap right palms together.
   2) Partners slap backs of right hands together.
   3) Slap own thigh with right hand.
   4) Snap own right fingers.
   5) Repeat.

Partner Jive in *three*.
   1) Clap own hands.
   2) Partners clap right hands together.
   3) Partners clap left hands together.
   4) Repeat.

Partner Jive in *three*:
1) One partner reaches hands out toward other partner, with one hand at eye level (palm down), the other hand at hip level (palm up). The other partner mirrors this image, so both partners' right and left palms are touching. Clap hands together in this position.
2) Clap partner's hands straight out in front (palms facing toward partner).
3) Clap own hands.
4) Repeat.

Partner Jive in *six*:
1) Slap own legs.
2) Tap own shoulders.
3) Clap own hands.
4) Partners clap each other's right hands together.
5) Partners clap each other's left hands together.
6) Partners clap both hands together.
7) Repeat.

COLLABORATIVE METERS II

Keep those same partners. This time, while listening to music with a *meter in four*, partners face one another and repeatedly count aloud the four beats of each measure, throughout the duration of the music. Instruct them to clap each other's hands together *only* on specific beats. This activity helps students to accurately execute on-beat and syncopated rhythmic skills:

1) Only clap on beat one.

2) Only clap on beat three.

3) Only clap on beats one and three.

4) Only clap on beat four.

5) Only clap on beats one and four:

6) Only clap on beat two.

7) Only clap on beats two and four.

8) Only clap on beats two and four of the first measure, then on beats two and three of the second measure.

9) Only clap on beats four of the first measure, then on beats three and four of the second measure.

METER MADES

Remember the heartbeat page from the section titled "Beat Notations" on page 40? Using the very same page of heartbeats, the concept of meter is transferred from *drawing heartbeats*, to *drawing meter*. Play a recording of music with *meter in three*, for example. As children listen and determine the strong and weak pulses, encourage them to draw straight, vertical lines through the heartbeats as they did before. While listening to the recording a second time, the children can draw *long* lines through the strong heartbeats, and *short* lines through the weak beats. They are encouraged to draw bar lines after each set of three heartbeats, and, double bar lines at the end, and a number "three" at the beginning, as in this example:

Repeat this activity using recordings of music in various meters. Additional concepts such as: *measure, time signature, bar line* and *double bar line* are more easily introduced.

BOUNCING METERS

A meter strategy with a bouncing ball brings gym class to your music lesson! Children are arranged in a standing circle. While listening to a recording of music in a specified meter, children are encouraged to bounce the ball in one direction around the circle in this manner:

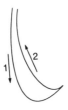

1) Child with the ball bounces it to the floor in front of adjacent child on left side on beat *one*.
2) Adjacent child catches ball and pats it for the remaining beats in the meter.
3) Same child bounces ball to the floor in front of next child on beat *two*, going in same direction, and so on.
4) Continue this activity throughout the duration of the recording, making sure that each child has a turn.

BRAVO, MAESTRO!

Show conducting patterns in various meters drawn on the chalkboard or large charts. Have students practice conducting the meters "in the air" while counting aloud. When a conducting pattern is established, play a recording in a selected meter, and allow students to determine the meter by focusing their listening on the strong and weak beats in each set. They can conduct the music, using woodsticks as "batons."

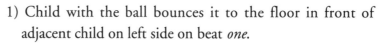

Meter in 2   Meter in 3   Meter in 4

METER BINGO

1) Give each student a reproduced page of 25 "Bingo" squares and a pencil.

2) Designate a meter.

3) Draw 24 game rhythms in a designated meter at the chalkboard or large chart.

4) Students identify the centermost square on their Bingo page as the FREE SPACE.

5) Students copy the rhythms at the chalkboard into the squares of their Bingo page, in random order. (Each Bingo page is then unique.)

6) Clap out a selected rhythm at the chalkboard. Students echo-clap back.

7) Draw an X by the clapped rhythm at the chalkboard. Students search their Bingo pages for same rhythm, and draw an X in the square which shows it.

8) Continue game in same manner. When a "BINGO" is completed on a student's Bingo page (a row of X squares which runs vertically, horizontally, diagonally, or four corners and the FREE SPACE), that student calls: "Bingo!"

9) The student who completed Bingo must call back the rhythms to verify that they were indeed called and clapped. Check these against the marked rhythms at the chalkboard.

10) This student becomes the new rhythm clapper, the game continues where it left off, or an entirely new game can begin.

METER PRACTICE PAGE

Design a meter "practice page" which includes several, four-measure rhythm sequences in various meters. Number each example. Reproduce and distribute to students. Clap one of the examples, stressing the strong beats. Students search for the rhythm, and identify the number of the example. Allow students to clap the rhythms for one another.

FIND THE HIDDEN SONG

1) Select a favorite song which students could recognize just from its rhythmic notation.

2) Create a "practice page" with enough blank measures for the entire song, and eight more measures. Include the time signature of the selected song.

3) Fill in every two or three measures with rhythms from the selected song in the correct sequence. (The song is notated in sequence, but interrupted with eight blank measures throughout.)

4) Fill in the remaining measures with rhythms in contrasting meters, but do not add time signatures.

5) Reproduce and distribute with pencils to students.

6) Instruct students to notice the time signature, and cross out the *wrong* measures which contain an incorrect number of beats.

7) Students clap out the remaining rhythms, and guess the title to the "mystery song!"

STRATEGIES FOR
TEACHING PHRASE

FOLLOW THE RAINBOW

To help bring the concept of *phrase* to a conscious level, ask children to sing a known song with you while at the same time counting the number of times during the song that you take a breath. (Be sure to take a slightly-exaggerated breath prior to each phrase of words, in order to highlight this concept.) "How many breaths did we take?" Help students discover the correct number this way: Repeat the song, while having a student draw a "rainbow" (phrase marking) at the chalkboard or large chart for each inhalation. (If there are eight breaths, there are eight left-to-right rainbows.) Students count the number of phrase markings.

To transfer the concept, invite students to sing a different song with you, this time drawing the "rainbows" in the air with you, and counting the number.

MOVING PHRASES

• Students create and perform a different motion for each phrase of a simple round or canon. Each phrase of words is visually highlighted with the separate, accompanying motion.

• Transfer the concept of phrase by selecting a different round or canon, and singing each phrase of words to a separate wall of the music room. Each wall represents one phrase of music.

STRATEGIES FOR TEACHING
PITCH AND MELODY

SOUND MAPS

Make non-musical, vocal tones, in a variety of pitches, like: a plane taking off, a siren, a firework, a doorbell, etc. As the tones are sounding, draw a "sound map" at the chalkboard or large chart that visually describes the aural message, showing up and down tones, or tones which repeat. Trace over the sound map as children echo the same tones. Children can draw their own sound maps to accompany their own improvised vocal tones, and the teacher can echo. For example:

HIGH AND LOW

• Very young children are easily confused with the melodic concept of *high* and *low*, because they often falsely interpret high and low to be qualities of volume, not pitch. When children are requested by others to "turn *down* the radio," the concept of "down" means to make the volume *softer*. Conversely, to "turn *up* the radio" means to make the volume *louder*. Sensitive music teachers can take extra care in reinforcing the correct translation of *up* and *down* to: *high* and *low* pitch.

• Emphasize gross differences in high and low pitch by playing familiar melodies up high in the treble, or down low in the bass. Invite students to respond physically by pointing up or down. Gradually make the intervalic distance smaller by playing the melodies only an octave apart, a seventh apart, a sixth apart, a fifth apart, etc.

▶ **"When students can distinguish the highness or lowness of entire melodies, challenge them to distinguish the highness or lowness of single pitches."**

• When students can distinguish the highness or lowness of entire melodies, challenge them to distinguish the highness or lowness of single pitches. Have two separately-pitched resonator bells hidden from view. Play one bell. Then, upon playing the second bell, ask students to determine if the sound is higher or lower than the original bell. Begin this activity with bells pitched quite far apart. Continue the activity by gradually replacing the bells with ones which are pitched closer and closer to one another, until the two bells are pitched only a half-step apart.

Note: For individual fun, place a standing, blindfolded student in between two others holding the two resonator bells. The students holding the resonator bells play them individually. The blindfolded student must guess which bell played "high" and which bell played "low."

• For more challenge, obtain two bells pitched the same, and another pitched higher or lower. While hidden from view, play the three bells, and ask students to determine which two bells sounded alike, and which one sounded different. *"Did the different bell sound higher or lower than the original bell?"* As in the above activity, begin with bells pitched quite far apart, gradually decreasing the size of the interval. Show the bells and correlate the size of the bell to the highness or lowness of pitch it produced.

ROCKIN' BODY RHYTHMS

Say "Hi" to the Music Staff! When children know their basic rhythm patterns, instead of introducing the staff with melody patterns, first expose them to the concept of high-low on the staff by using the rhythms they've already learned with body-percussion sounds. Label a treble staff, and create a body-percussion piece that, when notated on the staff, is just difficult enough to challenge your children's music-reading skills, or use *Rockin' Body Rhythms* on page 61. Note that the highest sound (finger snaps) is notated on the top line of the staff, while conversely, the lowest sound (foot stomp) is notated on the bottom line. These rhythms have melodic directionality, as they are both notated and performed *high* and *low*.

ROCKIN' BODY RHYTHMS - 1

ROCKIN' BODY RHYTHMS - 2

CONSIDER THE SOURCE

Students can practice ear-training by echo-singing single pitches and combinations of pitches. Whether they identify pitches with numbers or solfege doesn't matter. Vary the sound source of the original melody. For example, instead of always *singing* melodic examples for your students to echo, consider *playing* them on the recorder, bamboo flute, guitar, song bells, xylophone, metallophone, glockenspiel, piano, and more.

MATCH MY PITCH

Getting students "tuned up" at the beginning of the music lesson can be achieved with this simple, focused listening strategy. Sing or hum a pitch and invite each student in turn to sing or hum it with you. It only takes a few seconds for the tone to travel around the room. When each one has sounded the tone, he/she keeps sounding it, taking intermittent breaths when necessary. When the entire group is sounding the tone, cut it off. You can determine very quickly which children have success or difficulty matching pitch.

For an extension of the above activity use combinations of pitches, for example: *sol, fa, mi, re, do.* When the last tone, *do*, is sounded and held, the next student in turn sings the same melody and holds the last tone, and so on. It is quite easy to evaluate which students are having success or difficulty with matching simple melodic sequences.

HIGH-STEPPIN'

A wooden, cardboard, or styrofoam "staircase" on which to place song bells, comes in handy when analyzing the visual, stepwise relationship of pitches to one another. It is also an excellent way to illustrate the concept of melodic directionality, i.e. "music sounding higher" and "music sounding lower." With a stepladder, the bells are played in upward and downward motions, and the concept of directionality — tones sounding higher and lower, is visually reinforced.

MUSICAL FAMILY MEMBERS

When introducing the relationship of single pitches to one another, or melodic phrases, strive to show them in context of the scale from which they are taken. A staff-lined chart or chalkboard might show the new pitch or phrase notated in one color, and the remaining notes of the scale in a contrasting color. This visual demonstration serves to help students relate the parts (new pitches) to the whole (scale). Use this strategy with all scales: major, minor, pentatonic, whole-tone, diatonic and chromatic.

THE THUMBS HAVE IT

When children are being asked to identify a melodic concept, such as *upward/downward directionality*, display a staff-lined chart which shows the correctly notated melodic example. Sing or play the example correctly, or deliberately incorrectly. Children can respond to the aural example with a show of thumbs: "thumbs up" evaluates a correct performance; "thumbs down" evaluates an incorrect performance. Or, children may respond: "Right on, honey!" or, "No way, baby!"

RELATIVELY SPEAKING

When introducing a new pitch, for example: *"la,"* highlight its aural relationship with previously learned pitches *"sol"* and *"mi."* Demonstrating with three hidden song bells, play the two learned pitches, then play the new pitch. Probe students' listening: "Does the new pitch sound higher or lower than the learned pitches?" Introduce the new pitch on a staff, showing its visual relationship with the learned pitches, *"sol"* and *"mi."*

LEADING THE WITNESS

Work the ears harder than the voice. It's the challenge of ear-training. When students have learned the concept of eight sequential pitches in the major scale, have them practice singing the pitches with you like this: You sing *do*, they sing *re*. You sing *mi*, they sing *fa*, and so on. When students hear your pitch, their inner ear is challenged to hear the next pitch in the sequence before sounding it. The concept is extended with use of other musical scales: pentatonic, minor, whole tone, diatonic and chromatic.

THREE-WAY MELODIES

1) In this three-way melody echo, have students pair into partners, each pair sharing a set of song bells.
2) Designate one partner to be the "echo," the other, the "player."
3) Sing a simple melodic phrase, appropriate for the learning level of your students.
4) The "echoes" echo-sing the melodic phrase, immediately followed by the "players," who play it on the bells.
5) Do several melodic phrases.
6) Partners switch roles and the activity repeats.

MYSTERY MEASURE

1) Select, or compose a four measure melody.

2) Notate the music, all except the last measure on a large staff-lined chart or chalkboard, for viewing.

3) On a separate chart, notate the last measure, and include three other, alternative measures of contrasting "endings." Label: "Ending #1, Ending #2, Ending #3, and Ending #4."

4) Play or sing the entire four measures of melody.

5) Students are challenged to identify the correct ending measure.

6) Play again, this time using an alternating measure. Students identify.

7) This activity can be adapted for rhythm.

NAME THAT TUNE

1) Select six to eight known songs.

2) Print each song title on a separate flash card.

3) During music class, choose individual students to hold the flashcards in view.

4) Play any phrase from any of the songs, on piano, recorder, guitar, song bells, etc. It does not have to be the opening phrase of the song, such as in the familiar game, "Name That Tune."

5) Remaining students attempt to identify the correct song title by naming the student holding the correct card.

Another strategic variation on "Name That Tune":

1) Arrange music class into two groups.

2) Students in each group are numbered for order of response.

3) Determine the starting group.

4) Play or sing the first pitch of a "mystery tune." (It is truly an incredible feat for any student to correctly name the mystery tune given this meager bit of information, and the author suspects that mental telepathy is at work.)

5) The starting member of the starting team attempts to name the mystery tune. If unable, the turn goes to the other group.

6) Play or sing the first and second pitches of the mystery tune.

7) The starting player of the other group attempts to name the mystery tune. If the mystery tune is correctly named, two points are earned for that team, and the turn returns to the original group.

8) A new "mystery tune" is selected, and a new round begins. Continue to add on as many pitches for clues as necessary until the mystery tune is correctly named. Turns ALWAYS alternate between the two groups. The number of points awarded to a group is the number of pitches it took to correctly identify the mystery tune.

Determine a set number of points that if accumulated, enable the entire group to receive a grand prize, such as stickers, hand stamps, a favorite recording or song, a favorite video, or popcorn party, etc.

INSIDE-OUT MELODIES

Need a strategy to introduce the concept of sight-singing? Start with something familiar:

1) Select a familiar song with a simple melody. Good choices are: *Are You Sleeping, Twinkle Twinkle Little Star, This Old Man*, and the like.
2) Notate each phrase of the song on treble staff-lined flash cards, and include lyrics.
3) Invite your singers to sing the song so that the tune is inside their inner ears (musical memory).
4) Scramble the flash cards and set them on a ledge. Lead your singers through the scrambled song, striving for in-tune singing as they sight-sing the melody exactly as it appears. The challenge is to sing the starting pitch on each flash card accurately; the remaining notes in the measure are easily recalled. Children say: "The song sounds inside out!"

SCRAMBLED EGGS

Here's a cooperative-learning group strategy that reinforces melodic note-reading:

1) Choose four to six known songs.
2) For each song, notate the first four or eight measures of melody (without lyrics) on treble, staff-lined cards, one measure per card.
3) On the reverse side of each card, print each song title. (If card sets are of contrasting colors, organization is more efficient.)
4) Make enough sets of cards for each cooperative-learning group. (Label the reverse side of each card set: A, B, C, etc. to correspond with each cooperative-learning group.)
5) List song titles at the chalk-board.

6) Invite students to sing a selected song (the four to eight notated measures, that is) while clapping the rhythm.

7) Place a set of melody cards face-down and scrambled to each student group. The song title is visible on the reverse side of the cards.

8) Designate a time limit, say one minute.

9) At your signal, students arrange the cards into the correct melodic sequence. Groups that correctly sequence the cards within the designated time, earn one point each.

10) Continue the activity with remaining sets of cards.

11) Having a pre-determined number of points eligible for a grand prize, tally up the total number of points earned by the entire class. (A grand prize could be a favorite song or game at the end of music class, stickers or stamps on the hand, a favorite video or record, popcorn party, etc.)

COUCH POTATOES

Since the invention of television, advertizers have used classic musical themes in their commercials. Obtain recordings of some "commercial themes" currently being heard on TV. When children hear such a melody in music class, they are usually quick to note that it is the music to an oft-seen commercial. With the aid of a composer's biography and picture, children can learn "fun facts" about the musical source of their favorite commercial melody!

KEYBOARD EXTRAVAGANZA

How many times have your students asked to bring to music class their portable, electronic keyboards? These keyboards are perfect for a unit on melody singing and playing. Arrange a date, and send home a note with instructions:

1) Keyboard must be in operating condition.
2) Student must know how to operate the keyboard.
3) Batteries, battery pack or cord must be included.

Children without keyboards may play song bells, or other available, pitched instruments. The ensemble sound is truly unique!

MOOD MUSIC

It's often fun to demonstrate the emotional impact which melodic range, pitch, rhythm and dynamics have on the listener's perception. Play recordings of *Jaws*, by John Williams; *Morning Mood*, from *Peer Gynt Suite No.1*, by Edward Grieg; *Cradle Song*, by Johannes Brahms; *Fertility of the Earth* from *The Rite of Spring* by Igor Stravinsky; *E.T.*, by John Williams. Think of other movie themes, or program music which set a mood or tell a story.

LIP-SYNC ARTISTS

More than ever before, music publishers are supplying accompaniment cassette tapes along with song materials. One side of the tape features the accompaniment only, the reverse side features voices plus accompaniment. When note-reading is basically achieved, allow your singers to "lip sync," or sing along with the taped voices, only for the purpose of connecting the aural sound with the written notes. This strategy is an excellent one for helping children follow musical notation, but must be used judiciously. Children singers who are allowed to rely on taped performances when learning to sing melodies, are often content to let their inner ears become lazy. Children can inadvertently miss a valuable learning experience if the professionally-recorded singers are allowed to do most of the singing.

STRATEGIES FOR TEACHING HARMONY

HARMONY IN STEREO

The concept of part-singing is easily introduced with this *harmony* strategy. Teach children a simple chant or nursery rhyme. Divide children into two or three groups. While maintaining a steady beat (patting heart or slapping thighs), one group recites the chant and is followed in canon by the remaining group(s) who enter one beat, one measure, or one phrase later. Tell children that since they own two ears, one ear listens to themselves; the other ear listens to the other group, simultaneously.

A FORGOTTEN VOICE

Many music teachers take attendance and overlook the tape recorder, yet it serves as a functional "voice" within the music lesson! When children are learning to sing in harmony, record them singing one part. While they sing another part, let the tape play at a barely audible level. With each subsequent rehearsal, increase the volume of the recording, until children are cognizant of harmonizing with the singers on the tape recorder. In a gradual way, children's ears become accustomed to successful part-singing, and they are soon able to sing in parts, sans the tape recorder!

PARTNER SONGS

Partner songs, when sung simultaneously, expose two, separate melodies to the listening ear. They are excellent choices for developing independent part-singing. The following partner songs harmonize well when sung together:

1) *When the Saints Go Marching In* and *Good Night Ladies*
2) *He's Got the Whole World in His Hands* and *Go Tell Aunt Rhody*
3) *The Farmer in the Dell* and *Here We Go Looby Loo*
4) *Merrily We Roll Along* and *London Bridge*
5) *She'll Be Comin' Round the Mountain* and *When the Saints Go Marching In*
6) *Skip to My Lou* and *Rock-a-My Soul*
7) *Here We Go Round the Mulberry Bush* and *Oh Dear, What Can the Matter Be*
8) *Three Blind Mice* and *Row Row Row Your Boat* and *Are You Sleeping*
9) *This Train* and *When the Saints Go Marching In*

SOUNDS AROUND

While your singers sing the melody to a song, walk among and around them, singing the harmony part by yourself. Next, add two singers to your "team." Sing again. Add four more voices, and so on, until the growing harmony settles into your singers' ears and voices.

STEPPING IN TUNE

Once harmony is achieved with a two or three-part canon or round, or partner song, assemble standing singers into two or three concentric circles. Each group walks the beat, in the opposite direction of adjacent circles, while singing the designated harmony part. The concept of harmony is visually reinforced.

FIND THE HIDDEN TONE

Harmonizing involves tuning up the *ear* more than the *voice!*
Practice tuning up a music group involved in part-singing with
this harmony strategy. Play a three-note chord at the piano.
With their "inner ear," ask your singers to mentally discern the
lowest tone of the triad. Sing it. Discern the highest tone. Sing
it. Discern the middle tone. Sing it. Change chords and repeat.

A MINOR TECHNICALITY

• Here's a harmony switch. Sing songs with a *major* tonality in
the *minor* mode. Imagine *Yankee Doodle, For He's a Jolly Good
Fellow,* or *Joy to the World* sung in a minor key. To further
illustrate the difference in tonalities, sing *Are You Sleeping,* then
listen to *Symphony #1 in D Major, Fourth Movement,* by Gustav
Mahler. The music sounds the same theme, but within a minor tonal setting.
Compare both musical experiences.

• In contrast, select songs notorious for their minor tonality, such as
Halloween songs, or funeral marches, and cheer them up by singing or
playing them in a major key. Invite students to share their reactions upon
hearing known melodies accompanied with contrasting harmonies.

TUNES FOR STRUMMIN'

Let's introduce chords. For starters, choose a simple, two chord folk song
such as *O Susannah,* by Stephen Foster, and invite students to sing it while
you accompany with autoharp or guitar. Explain that three or more tones
sounding together simultateously, such as when the strings are strummed,
create a musical chord. Suggest that students watch the chord bars, and note
on which *words* the chord changes occur. Repeat the song, this time having
students push an imaginary *"do"* chord on their right knee with left hand
while "strumming" imaginary strings with the right hand. Push the *"sol"*
chord on the left knee with the left hand. Repeat, but leave out the
accompaniment, and see if student's "inner ears" can tell when to change
knees for the correct harmony. Allow students to take turns playing the
autoharp accompaniment.

S T R A T E G I E S   F O R
TEACHING TEMPO

SPEED OF THE HEARTBEAT

Children's heartbeats average approximately 80 beats per minute. Children exposed to music with a *tempo* of less than 80 beats per minute experience a sedative effect. Music with a tempo of more than 80 beats per minute provides stimulation.

A LOOK AT TEMPO

Prepare fun posters which reinforce the concept of tempo. Find pictures of animals, or machines that move in varying degrees of fast and slow:

1) Mount the picture on the poster.
2) Add a catchy caption or quote.
3) Add tempo term.
4) Add translation.

For example, a picture of a turtle is captioned: "WHAT'S THE HURRY?" accompanied by the tempo term *largo* (translated – very slow).

CHOOSE YOUR TEMPO

• List several tempo terms on a large chart or chalkboard. For instance: *allegro, moderato, andante, largo*, etc. Select a familiar song and sing it at each of these tempos to help reinforce the concept of fast and slow music, and how choices of tempo can be appropriate or not appropriate for certain styles of music.

• Later, hold a ticking, hand-held metronome, or have one ticking in the classroom as music students enter. Choose a tempo indication, ♩=72, for example, and discover the speed of the beat. Choose several tempos, and analyze the relationship between the number of beats per minute, and the relative degree of speed, by singing a known song at varying tempi.

READY, SET, GO!

When leading children in the singing of songs, establish the tempo and starting pitch with this simple strategic invitation. Be sure to sing on the starting pitch of the song, and sing in the appropriate tempo of the song: "One, two, ready, begin."

COLLECTIVE DECISION

Students can collaboratively lead themselves to begin singing with this tempo strategy. Encourage students to concentrate on the approximate tempo of the song to be performed. Invite them to tap two fingers into the opposite palm, all at the same time, to a steady beat, while striving to agree on the same tempo. At first, the taps sound at varying tempi, and gradually come together, merging into one, collective tempo. When that tempo is established, a designated student calls: "One, two, ready, begin."

STRATEGIES FOR TEACHING STYLE

RIGHT IN STYLE

Obtain recordings of various styles of the same music, for instance, the holiday song, *White Christmas*, by Irving Berlin. Play recordings which feature the song performed by a male or female vocal soloist, duet, trio, quartet or ensemble of singers. Other recordings could feature instrumental performances: jazz combo, string orchestra, concert band, marching band, and more. Ask specific questions relative to style, to generate thinking responses, such as:

"How many different instruments do you hear?"
"How many instruments can you name?"
"Was there any change in dynamics between one recording and the next?"
"Did the form change at all between recordings?"
"Did any singers or instrumentalists improvise on the melody?"
"Describe the kind of harmony. Does harmony occur with canon, with chords, with a descant, with multiple voices?"

SAME SONG, NEW STYLE

This strategy is a favorite, because it involves a lot of "brainstorming" and the possibilities for successful learning outcomes are limitless! Transform the "character" (mood, tone, personality) of a known song by changing different elements of its style. As you experiment with each one of these strategies, ask, "What effect is achieved if we..."

1) Change the tempo from slow to fast, or vice versa.
2) Change the meter from "three beats per measure" to "four beats per measure," or vice versa.
3) Change the tonality from major to minor, or vice versa.
4) Change the melody from high range to low range, or vice versa.
5) Change the dynamics from loud to soft, or vice versa.
6) Change the tone color as desired by changing instruments and/or ranges and numbers of voices.
7) Change the rhythmic structure from simple eighth notes to dotted eighth and sixteenth notes for a swing feel.

This activity always culminates in shared smiles and giggles as all-too-familiar songs take on brand new identities. Hint: Accompany songs with an electronic keyboard equipped to vary the tempo, range, percussion accompaniment, meter, harmony (chords), volume and tone color.

CONTRASTING STYLES

Invite students to brainstorm as many musical styles as possible, and listen to recordings which exemplify each one. Compare recordings in terms of the basic musical elements: rhythm, melody, harmony, form, tempo, dynamics and tone color. Ask lots of questions to generate thinking responses. Some styles to think about are:

1) Period styles – Renaissance, Baroque, Classical, Romantic, and Contemporary.
2) Dance styles – allemande, gigue, minuet, gavotte, march, tarantella, polka and more.
3) Popular styles – swing, dixieland, blues, bluegrass, gospel, country, jazz, rock, rock and roll, soul, fusion, reggae and more.

STRATEGIES FOR
TEACHING DYNAMICS

MUSIC THAT'S OUT OF THIS WORLD

It's easiest and most natural for students of all ages to experience dynamic contrasts in music before being formally introduced to the Italian terms. For very young students, use this simple game strategy to reinforce the concept of changing volume in music:

1) Obtain a small "star" ornament, or cut out a small, paper star.

2) Designate one student to be the "astronaut" – the one who "flies to outer space to catch a shooting star." This student waits outside the classroom.

3) Designate another student to hide the star anywhere in the classroom, as long as it is in plain sight. For example, the star cannot be placed under a book, or up high on a bookshelf out of reach.

4) Invite the "astronaut" back into the classroom with this chant: "Ten, nine, eight, seven, six, five, four, three, two, one, ignition, blast-off!"

5) The "astronaut" enters the room (outer space) and walks about in search of the "shooting star," while remaining students repeatedly sing *Twinkle Twinkle Little Star*.

6) As the "astronaut" moves, the children's singing gives clues as to proximity of the star by getting louder as he/she approaches the star, or softer as he/she moves away from the star.

7) At last, when the "astronaut" locates the star, applause is given, and the student who hid the star becomes the new "astronaut" while the previous "astronaut" chooses a new student to hide the star. The game begins again.

A LOOK AT DYNAMICS

STILL Bulletin Board

Create your own poster or flashcards about *loud* and *soft* by locating magazine pictures of six animals that make loud or soft sounds. Cleverly arrange the pictures on a poster, caption each one, add the Italian term and translation. For example, a picture of a lion roaring might be captioned: "I'M THE LOUD MOUTH AROUND HERE!" The Italian term is *fortissimo*, and the translation is *very loud*. Include these dynamic levels:

pianissimo = very soft
piano = soft
mezzo piano = medium soft
mezzo forte = medium loud
forte = loud
fortissimo = very loud

VOLUME DIAL

Construct a "volume dial" from a large piece of heavy-weight paper:

1) Draw a large circle.
2) On the background, label degrees of volume from one to ten around the circle, like a radio.
3) On the background, label the "ON-OFF" position, next to the "one" position.
4) Cut out an appropriately-sized "dial" with an arrowhead at one end. Cut a small slot in opposite end.
5) Attach slot end of dial loosely to center of the circle with a brass brad, so arrowhead is pointed away from the center, and can be turned around the circle with ease.
6) Have students tap heartbeat while singing a familiar song. Throughout the song, turn the volume dial so that it points to varying degrees of volume. Students adjust their own singing volume accordingly.
7) At some point during the song, turn the dial to the OFF position. Inaudible singing continues, with the tapping heartbeats being the only audible sound. Turn the dial back ON, and students resume audible singing.

RIGHT BEFORE YOUR VERY EYES

Obtain a basketball, soccer ball or football (depending on season) for use as a volume prop. While children sing a known song and pat the heartbeat, hold the ball directly in front to elicit maximum volume. As you move the ball to the side, the singing volume fades. When the ball is held behind your back, audible singing ceases, but the song silently continues. When the ball is moved out front again, audible singing resumes.

DYNAMICS COME IN HANDY

When a very young child is asked how "big," or loud a sound is, the response is typically punctuated with outstretched arms. Use this childlike gesture to elicit dynamic contrasts from singers. While singing a known song or listening to a recording with wide dynamic contrasts, invite students to describe the volume level according to the amount of space between their outstretched hands. Hands cupped close together designate minimal volume; hands pulled far apart designate maximum volume.

LOUD AND SOFT DRAMA

"As quiet as a mouse..." Locate pictures, or draw words at the chalkboard of things, animals or motions that make soft sounds, such as a kitten, car blinker, ticking metronome or clock, mouse, puppy, snake, leaves falling, tip-toe, chewing, bird flapping wings, typing on a computer, etc. Play a recording of soft music, while showing a "quiet picture." (or "quiet word" at the chalkboard). Children assemble in free formation about the room, and dramatize improvised motions which visually describe the "quiet" thing. Do same activity with the concept: *loud.*

THE PIANOFORTE

This is a story-telling strategy that helps reinforce the concept of dynamic contrast. Ahead of time, obtain recordings of:

1) Clavichord or harpsichord music from the Baroque era, by Handel, Purcell or Bach.
2) A recording of a piano piece with a wide dynamic contrast, such as *Piano Sonata in D minor Op. 31, No. 2, (The Tempest), First Movement,* by Ludwig Van Beethoven.
3) Pictures or illustrations which show the comparative features of the clavichord, harpsichord and piano.

During the lesson, tell this story:

1) Early keyboard instruments had the capacity to sound at only one volume. The clavichord (the grandfather of the piano) used wood tangents that popped up to strike the strings. Demonstrate with a recording and illustration.
2) The harpsichord (the father of the piano) used quills that plucked the strings. Demonstrate with a recording and illustration.

3) Then, in the year 1709, the pianoforte was invented by Bartolomeo Christofori, and it used hammers which popped up to strike the strings. The player could make the hammers strike the strings quickly (making a *loud* sound), or slowly (making a *soft* sound). That is why the instrument was named *pianoforte*. In time, this instrument came to be known as the piano. Play the recording of the Beethoven piano sonata, or other selected piano piece.

SINGING THAT FITS

Instead of requesting that students sing louder (this promotes a tendency to drive the voice), try asking them to sing with a *bigger* voice. Conversely, students may be asked to sing with a *smaller* voice, as opposed to singing softer.

HI-TECH DYNAMICS

Call upon that assistant music teacher, the tape recorder, for this strategy. Select a familiar song which has the capacity for a wide contrast of dynamic levels. Invite students to sing the song while maintaining a consistent, medium-loud dynamic level. Record this performance on cassette tape. Listen to the play-back, and manipulate the volume control to increase or decrease the volume as directed by the students. If more or less volume is desired, a "thumbs up" or "thumbs down" signal is used. Visually reinforce dynamic choices with flashcards, as described on page 74.

STRATEGIES FOR
TEACHING TONE COLOR

MEETING THE RHYTHM BAND

Are the children just beginning to become friends with rhythm instruments? Arrange children in a seated circle, and give each one a rhythm instrument. Play eight beats of a march at the piano, or play a recording, while students play a steady beat on their instrument. Stop the music, and instruct each child to pass his/her instrument to the adjacent child on the right. The instruments are passed while all chant:

"Two, four, six, eight.
Pass it on, now don't be late!"

Continue the activity, until children have had a turn to experiment with the *tone color* of each instrument.

FOCUSED LISTENING

This tone-color strategy reinforces focused-listening skills:

1) Have students select four classroom instruments which produce contrasting *tone-colors*. For example, maracas, hand drum, tone block and resonator bell.
2) Designate four students to play the instruments.
3) Instruct remaining students to arrange themselves in a sitting, free formation, and close their eyes.
4) Conduct one player to play his/her instrument. As sitting students are concentrating on the sound, tell them that the tone color of that instrument is really a signal to move forward. Repeat this step with the remaining three instruments, assigning each a direction of reverse, to the right, and to the left.
5) Instruct sitting students to stand, and notice the friends who are standing nearby. Close eyes. Tell them that when they hear a particular tone color, they move in the designated direction, using small "baby steps."

6) Conduct a player to play his/her instrument. If that particular tone color is the signal for say, reverse, all students move in a backward direction, until you conduct the player to stop. When the sound stops, so do the movements.

7) Continue the activity by conducting the other players on their instruments. The moving students respond by moving in the designated direction. Occasionally, a moving student is unable to remember the correct direction in which to move, and bumps into another. This happens often, giggles occur, and, students are reminded to step away and continue moving in very small steps in the appropriate direction.

8) When movement in many directions has been achieved, stop the activity, and instruct students to open their eyes. Surprise! Are they standing near the same students as when the activity began? How well did the student's ears tell their feet where to move?

POP BOTTLE SYMPHONY

How about a "Pop Bottle Symphony" to assist with melodic note-reading? The tinkling tone colors add a new dimension to classroom instrumental ensembles.

1) Obtain eight glass, juice or pop bottles of the same size and density.
2) Label each one with a piece of tape that designates a pitch of the major scale: *do, re, mi, fa, sol, la, ti, do.*
3) Fill each bottle with colored water (add few drops food color) to the appropriate level that, when struck with a spoon, produces the desired pitch.
4) Repeat the above three steps with two or more sets of juice bottles, so that every student in your music class has one bottle to play. (It's O.K. if there are more bottles of certain pitches.)
5. Obtain a set of metal spoons, one for each student.
6. Select public domain melodies (melodies which are not copyrighted) that use every pitch of the Major Scale. For example: *Three Blind Mice, Christmas is Coming, White Coral Bells,* etc. Notate the melody and above each pitch, print the Italian "nickname" (*do, re, mi,* etc.)
7. Reproduce copies of the melodies and give one page to each student.
8. Conduct the ensemble of pop-bottle musicians through the entire melody, each student playing his/her bottle at the appropriate place in the melody.

MUSICAL PLACE SETTINGS

Keep those juice bottles handy. Add a knife/ fork set for each student, and the menu of available classroom tone colors grows. Call this activity "Project Create" and organize students into cooperative-learning groups.

1) Each group creates a 16-measure rhythm piece, designating certain measures to be played in these ways:
   a) B = knife strikes bottle
   b) F = knife strikes hand-held fork
   c) D = knife strikes desk (or floor)
2) Label each measure with either B, F, or D to indicate the manner of performance.
3) Add a repeat sign at the end, if necessary to increase length.
4) Each cooperative-group takes turns playing their "Project Create" accompaniment to a favorite recording, or piano piece performed by you or a student.

INSTRUMENT SLEUTH

(To be played after students have been introduced to the characteristic tone colors produced by many musical instruments)

1) Obtain a recording of individual, instrumental sounds.
2) Obtain pictures of instruments featured on the recording.
3) Attach a picture to the back of each student. (The fun part here is that students can see everyone's instrument except their own.)
4) Choose one student to be the Sleuth.
5) Listen to the first instrument on the recording.
6) While music is playing, the Sleuth walks among the remaining students, searching for the one who has the correct instrument on his/her back.
7) The Sleuth taps the selected student on the back, and the tapped student must identify the instrument on his/her own back.
8) This student is now the Sleuth and the game continues until each student has been tapped.

THE MYSTERY VOCALIST

Tone colors are not limited to instrumental sounds. Play this simple game during which very young children determine the vocal tone colors of friends' voices. One child is blindfolded. Another child is given a stuffed heart or cut-out paper heart to hold. All sing the song *Who Am I Thinkin' Of?* At the end, the child holding the heart sings the name of the blindfolded child on the *sol-mi* pitches. Allow the blindfolded child as many guesses as needed to correctly name the "mystery soloist." Play the game again, with the soloist taking the role of the blindfolded child, and the blindfolded child choosing the next soloist, etc.

"OOPS! I FORGOT TO GET INVENTED!"

For an outrageous music lesson, invite students to imagine that they are instrument designers hired to invent the musical instrument that "forgot to get invented." Post pictures of "already invented" instruments around the classroom within easy view. Discuss the moving parts of the instruments, and, the manner in which each is played in order to produce its sound. Imagine the newly-invented instrument to be played by humans, aliens, animals or others? Insist that the design of the instrument be thoroughly thought out, so that it is playable in a somewhat logical manner. It must include "moving parts" such as: keys, strings, bars, valves, slides; hammers, mallets, etc. It can be acoustic, electronic or solar, or anything else. Invite students to name the newly-invented instrument, and draw and color its design on paper, while music plays in the background. Share, discuss and laugh.

STRATEGIES FOR TEACHING
MOVEMENT AND DIRECTION

ECHOES, MIRRORS AND SHADOWS

An *echo* motion is one which happens after an original motion. A *mirror* motion is one which happens simultaneously with the original motion. Both of these strategies are used when introducing children to movement, with the teacher facing the children. Position children behind the teacher, and they *shadow* every motion in a synchronized manner.

OPPOSITES ATTRACT

When children face you and mirror your motions, remember to move with the *opposite* side of your body, so that they observe a mirror image of themselves. For example, if you instruct children to "step with your right foot," model that motion with your left foot, as you face them.

THE LADDER OF MOTIONS

Warm-up student's bodies for movement using the "ladder of motions." The "ladder of motions" consists of a series of flash cards placed in a ladder formation on the floor. Students stand around the ladder, so it is within view. On each flash card is printed a single movement, such as:

walk, hop, jog, gallop, skip, jump, run, scissors, hop-scotch, bounce, march, kick, swivel feet, knee bend, sway, slide, and more.

While listening to music with a beat, lead each of these motions to the beat of the music, beginning with the flash card on the bottom rung of the ladder, and ending on the top rung of the ladder. At a later lesson, allow a student to lead.

DANCING ON YOUR HANDS

This strategy breaks down a whole dance into its parts. Discover the form to the dance. On a chalkboard, or large chart, break down the dance steps into a visual description, showing part A, part B, etc. Within each section, notate the rhythm pattern of the feet, that is, the rhythmic patterns created by the actual sequence of steps. Before actually dancing to the music, invite students to tap the notated rhythm on the legs, with the left palm being the left foot, and right palm being the right foot, while counting the rhythm aloud. When students internalize the rhythm of the feet in this manner, they are prepared to transfer the fine-motor movement concepts to gross-motor movements of the feet and legs.

A BIRD'S EYE VIEW

Consider a bird's eye view of the classroom floor. Using the chalkboard or large chart, diagram dance movements and directionality as you demonstrate. This visual aid gives students one more angle from which to interpret your instructions.

UN-MARKED TEACHERS

When teaching difficult movements, discreetly place students who easily acquire the movements in front of, and between learning-challenged students, but only until movements are performed fairly confidently by all.

STRATEGIES FOR
TEACHING FORM

A MUSIC MAP

Describe the element of form as the map, blueprint or design of music.

FORM FLASH CARDS

Distribute flash cards to students on which these musical terms are printed: verse, refrain, bridge, coda, introduction, etc. Or use A, B, C, etc. Throughout the singing of a song that contains these elements of form, request students holding the cards to "pop up" when the element they are holding, occurs. To transfer the concept, sing a different song which contains the same elements of form, scramble the flash cards, and, invite students to sequence the cards into the correct order in which they occurred in the song.

RONDO FORM

Rondo form is easily introduced with this little, improvised rhythm game. For the "A" part, notate four measures of known rhythms, in any desired meter. Students all clap. For the "B" part, a selected student taps out four measures of improvised rhythm on a drum, tone block, tambourine or other percussion instrument. All students repeat the "A" rhythm. Parts "C," "D," etc. are improvised by remaining students in turn. (This game is easily adapted for teaching melody concepts, by substituting four measures of a notated melody for the rhythm measures, and by playing measures on song bells or other pitched instruments.)

SOUND SHEETS

Create your own personalized "sound sheets" upon which children can focus as they listen to selected recordings of music. Choose no more than two or three musical elements for highlighting. Design the "sound sheet" like a maze, or road map, in a left to right direction, with stopping points indicating where the highlighted elements occur in the music.

STRATEGIES FOR TEACHING INTERPRETIVE SYMBOLS AND TERMS

DO FIRST, SAY LATER

• When students meet a new interpretive symbol or term, such as a repeat sign, fermata, D.C.al fine, and others, refrain from explaining to them what to do musically. Instead, offer students your performance of the very concept, while they participate by following the notation. When finished, ask: "Now, what did that sign or symbol tell me to do with the music?"

TRANSLATION, PLEASE

Give some thought to creating an interpretive symbol/term dramatization. Students are the actors, and you are their director.

1) Notate eight measures of rhythm or melody patterns on flash cards, one measure per flash card.

2) Select the interpretive symbols or terms which your students are currently learning, and draw these on flash cards, one symbol/term per flash card. For example:

D.S. al Fine	𝄋	Fine

3) Choose eight students to hold the notated flash cards in a left-to-right sequence in front of the remaining students.

4) Choose other students to hold the interpretive symbol/term flash cards in selected positions within the sequence of students who are holding the notated flash cards.

5) As remaining students clap or sing the music on the notated flash cards, direct them to follow the *D.S. al Fine* flash card back to the 𝄋 flash card, and complete the performance at the *Fine* flash card.

6) Play again, but this time choose new student actors; change the positions of the interpretive symbol/term flash cards, and choose a student director in your place. The translation of interpretive symbols is more quickly internalized when children play act their meaning.

MUSICAL CHARADES

This activity is especially fun and humorous if played after several interpretive symbols and terms are learned.

1) On the chalkboard or large chart, draw all learned interpretive symbols and/or terms. Review their interpretations and/or functions.

2) Distribute pencils and paper to all.

3) Invite each student to create and print any sentence on the paper, and sign it.

4) Each student then selects one interpretive symbol/term and draws it above, below or to the side of the appropriate word in the sentence.

5) Determine the starting player. This student reads his/her sentence with the appropriate expression, style, tempo or form (as indicated by the interpretive symbol or term which he/she added). For example:

"Some of my baseball cards are very valuable."

mf ——————————— *fff*

(Student reads sentence at medium dynamic level, then speaks the word "valuable" in a very, very loud voice.)

‖: *"Some of my baseball cards are very valuable."* :‖

(Student repeats sentence.)

"Some of my baseball cards are very valuable."

rit.

(Student gradually slows down speech at the end of the sentence.)

6) Upon speaking the correct sentence, the speaker calls upon another student to identify the correct interpretive symbol/term.

7) This student identifies the interpretive symbol/term, then reads his/her sentence, and chooses another student to identify its correct interpretive symbol/term.

8) Each time a student correctly identifies the interpretive symbol or term, a point is earned for the entire group of students.

9) The game continues like a "round robin" until all the students have had a turn to speak their sentence, and identify the correct interpretive symbol/term from another student's sentence.

10) When a student has difficulty identifying the interpretive symbol/term, a friend may be chosen for assistance, although a point is not earned for that turn.

11) After having predetermined a number of points eligible for a group grand prize, tally the total number of earned points at the end of the game. A group grand prize might be stickers, stamps on the back of the hand, certificates, listening to a favorite recording or singing a favorite song.

5 ATTENTION GRABBERS

NO-FAIL FUNSTERS

When planning music lessons, music educators are reminded by colleagues and master teachers to "keep the child in our children." The focus of attention is always on what's best for the children, and rightfully so. But, what about some attention directed toward "what's best for the teacher?" How about some fun for the music teacher? Following are some enjoyable, techniques that can "put the child back in the grown-up!"

LET'S PRETEND

RAH! RAH! RAH!

To help students commit new musical terms to memory, pretend to be a cheerleader. Have a student print the musical term and/or accompanying symbol on the chalkboard. Using a megaphone prop, and a cheerleader-style voice, echo call the spelling of the term, while everyone claps an enthusiastic beat. For example:

> **"Keep the child in our children... Put the child back in the grown-up!"**

"ALLEGRO! Gimme an A! (Class echoes: 'A!') Gimme an L! (Echo) Gimme another L! (Echo) Gimme an E! (Echo) Gimme a G! (Echo) Gimme an R! (Echo) Gimme an O! (Echo) Whaddah ya got? (All: ALLEGRO!)"

LOOK WHO'S HERE - THE MYSTERY TEACHER

Dress up as one of the great composers when introducing the life story and/or music of that person. For example, a white, powdered wig can be can be rented at a party/costume shop. A dark sport coat and pants with white shirt can be accessorized with a length of wide lace, tucked into the collar, achieving the effect of an "ascot." The drama is fun for you and unforgettable for the children!

HAPPY BIRTHDAY, BEETHOVEN!

Celebrate birthdays of the great composers. Reproduce pictures of "birthday cake" which include the correct number of candles to show the current age (posthumous or living), and a small, biographical sketch of the composer's life, including notable musical works. Sing the birthday song, and pass out the "pieces of cake" for students to keep. If a student asks: "Why are we celebrating the birthday of a composer who happens to be dead?" Respond with:

"Even though a composer is not living, a part of him/her lives on forever – the music!"

ABRACADABRA!

• Short on tom-tom drums? While sitting on the floor, bend the knee of one leg, and pull the knee toward the chest. Place the foot flat on the floor, and hug the knee with the arm on the same side. Pat the knee with the opposite hand. Presto! A pretend drum!

• Introduce new instruments to students by pretending that they are human. For example:

"When the guitar gets up in the morning, he/she gets dressed with six strings. Notice the body, neck, and head of the guitar. It even has a mouth (sound hole) from which the singing comes. When it goes to sleep at night, it rests in the soft, velvet lined bed (guitar case)."

• Demonstrate the strumming technique used with guitar, autoharp and ukelele by pretending to wipe dirty fingernails onto clothes in repeated, steady, downward strokes.

THE VILLAIN

When student behavior gets mildly "out of hand," pretend to be "the bad guy" by playing the "villain theme music" on the piano. Using two-hand octaves, play the first three pitches of the minor scale: with this rhythm:

A PICTURE SAYS A THOUSAND WORDS

Help children visualize their physical act of singing in this humorous way. Locate magazine pictures of animals, fish, or birds which show the mouth posed in a variety of absurd positions: wide open, tightly shut, askew to one side, etc. Cut out pictures and mount on a large poster to which the caption is added: "What kind of singer are you? A JAW-BREAKER? Or, a HUM-DINGER?" Post on the inside of the classroom door, so it is visible as students enter/exit the room.

IMAGINE THAT

LOOK WHO'S DOING THE TEACHING

To reinforce the learning of a new music symbol, teach its correct term, but occasionally highlight the symbol by deliberately calling it by an incorrect name. For example, imagine:

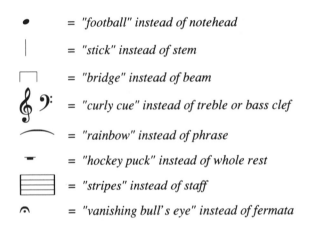

● = *"football" instead of notehead*

| = *"stick" instead of stem*

⌐ = *"bridge" instead of beam*

𝄞 𝄢 = *"curly cue" instead of treble or bass clef*

⌒ = *"rainbow" instead of phrase*

▬ = *"hockey puck" instead of whole rest*

▤ = *"stripes" instead of staff*

𝄐 = *"vanishing bull's eye" instead of fermata*

Instruct students to freely interrupt your teaching, if you should happen to "mis-term" any of these terms. Like this: students can chant together: *"No, NO! Mrs. Music Teacher, that's not a football, that's a notehead!"* Children love an opportunity to "correct" the teacher!

TEMPO TIME

It's story time, and the students are going to create the sound effects. The concept is tempo – the speed of the beat. Invite your students to tap a steady beat on their hearts, while you tell the story:

"Imagine that you are walking to school (medium fast beat). The sun is hot and you begin to tire (slower beat). The thought of eating tacos for lunch moves you forward (slightly faster beat). At school your name is announced over the public address system as having been selected "Student of the Year" (faster beat). In the principal's office you are awarded a certificate of honor and filmed by the local television station (very fast beat). After dinner, you call your friends to tell them to watch you on the evening new. (fast beat). It's night, and you snuggle under your covers for a good night's rest after a long, exciting day (slower beat). You fall asleep (very slow beat)."

MUSIC THAT'S DELICIOUS

Imagine that your lesson plan is a menu. When students ask, "What's on the menu for today?," you can describe the "appetizer" (review material), the "entre" or "meat and potatoes" (new material). Remember: Sometimes there are "dessert" choices (practice and play material) which can be suggested by the students, but only if "all the meat and potatoes are finished first!"

A TALENT SHOW

Suggest that students imagine the music room to be a concert hall. "Talent Day" can be presented during a regularly-scheduled music lesson as a special time during which students can share their unique musical talents with one another. All students are encouraged to share their favorite kind of musical involvement, not just the ones who take music lessons. Possiblities include favorite songs learned at summer camp, Sunday school, or home, improvising new lyrics to a familiar song, dramatizing a favorite song with motions and/or props, playing a favorite melody on an electronic keyboard, and more.

Run this event like a "talent show," with a student "master/mistress of ceremonies." The music room is divided into a "stage" area and an "audience" area. Rules of concert etiquette are maintained, such as applause before and after each performance and no talking during a performance. Certificates of participation are awarded to student performers.

MUSICAL PING-PONG

Play this "call and response" game by imagining the music room to be the site of a ping-pong match. Obtain a bean bag or a stuffed animal to toss as the "ping-pong ball." Randomly toss the bean bag to a student while singing a question, using the *sol-mi* pitches of the major scale. The student answers the question, attempting to sing on the same pitches, while tossing back the bean bag. Randomly toss it to another student, so that the bean bag moves back and forth rather quickly, and so on. Gradually, increase the "vocabulary" of pitches to include combinations of single pitches and intervals. This game is a fun way to encourage solo singing while at the same time relieving any accompanying anxiety.

WEE ONES

• For performance, instead of placing young children on the risers according to row 1, row 2, etc., imagine that each row is a cage at the zoo. The tallest row could be: "the giraffes," the next row: "the elephants," then "the bears," and finally, the shortest row: "the monkeys."

Note: Older students can label their riser rows from tallest to shortest this way: "quarters, dimes, nickels and pennies," to correspond with the largest to the smallest amounts of money.

• Young children are having difficulty forming a circle? At the beginning of the school year, place bits of colored, cloth tape in the floor to outline the circle. (Cloth tape is safe to use on floors.) As children practice forming a circle using the tape as a guide, gradually over time, take up some of the tape, until only a hint of the outline is visible. At a later date, remove all pieces of tape. Remind the children that the circle outline is still there: "It's right there in your mind's eye!"

• Young children can't remember to keep their space in a circle formation? Suggest that they imagine themselves to be pieces of a giant-sized circle puzzle. When the children concentrate on keeping every piece in its own special place, then the "puzzle is all put together."

• Very young children when asked to move from a standing position to a sitting position often "crash" to the floor. Play the imaginary "elevator" game by slowly descending to the floor, while singing this simple tune on the descending *sol-fa-mi-re-do* pitches of the major scale: (pretend to push the elevator button at each floor)

sol – Fifth floor, hardware.
fa – Fourth floor, ladies' wear.
mi – Third floor, mens' wear.
re – Second floor, childrens' wear.
do – First floor, we're there!

A FIVE STORY HOUSE

Introduce the music staff to children by imagining that it's a house with many floors: "Some music notes live way up high on the top floors, and some live on the middle floors, and some live way down low in the basement."

AUDIO TECHNICIANS

Rehearse a piece of music, by having students imagine that they are "tape recorders." Instruct them to "rewind" back to a particular measure, or "fast-forward" to another measure. "Play-back" is to perform, "pause" is to stop and listen, and "eject" is to put away the music.

FUN WITH

GADGETS AND MORE

• Battery-operated walkie-talkies or toy telephones that "work" are wonderful props used to reinforce the learning of new intervals and rhythmic/melodic patterns. Play an "echo-type" game, using known rhythms or melodies with the "leader" inside the classroom, and the "echo" outside the classroom, and vice versa. Take turns, and make sure all children have a chance to play with the props.

• Toy microphones are another prop that can be used effectively to conduct an "echo-type" activity. The "leader" points the microphone at him/herself while performing the original music, then points the microphone in the direction of the student(s) who perform the "echo."

• Wind-up music boxes or toy trains visually illustrate the concept of tempo. For example, while a wind-up train is chugging around the music room, gradually decreasing in speed, show a chart with this visual description of tempo. Later, apply the same concept chart to a piece of music.

Music getting faster: ♥ ♥ ♥ ♥ ♥♥♥♥

Music getting slower: ♥♥♥♥ ♥ ♥ ♥ ♥

• In advance, set 3-4 alarm clocks to sound within several minutes of each other. Using two toy telephones as props, ask a student to pick up one of the telephones and "answer it" when it "rings." (Turn off the alarm.) Pick up the other telephone and sing a conversation using the *sol-mi* pitches of the major scale with the student on the first telephone. Use combinations of pitches and intervals. Improvise new conversations with other students when the other telephones "ring."

• A cooperative-learning group of students has one child with a "gabby-mouth"? Instead of simply reminding children to speak in turns, give each child five tokens. At each speaking turn, a child places a token in the center of the group. If he/she discovers that all five tokens are in the center, he/she is to refrain from speaking until all other children's tokens are also in the center. The tokens promote a sense of "fair play," by visually reminding a child of his/her number of "speaking turns."

SEEING THE WHITES OF THEIR EYES

How many times have you had to remind your singers to keep their eyes focused on you, while directing them from the piano? Find a magazine picture of a frog, ostrich, or other animal with oversized eyes, and mount it on a poster. Put "sticky tack" in the top two corners on the backside of the poster. Keep it handy in the piano bench and bring it out and post it on the piano where singers can see it as a reminder to "keep watching." Reward the singers with a prize for a pre-determined number of rehearsals during which they can keep the frog in the piano bench.

STUFFED MUSIC FRIENDS

• A favorite stuffed animal can coax a shy participant. If a child is hesitant about leaving his/her space in order to take a turn, simply place the stuffed animal in his/her space to "guard your space, and keep it safe and warm until you return." The student may wish to hold the stuffed animal for a little while longer. This little maneuver also keeps the child from forgetting where his/her space is located.

• Small children in your music class are just beginning to find their singing voices. Many of them are are shy, or, "sing" in a monotone range. Make or obtain two puppets. Let the students name them. Dramatize a singing lesson in which you manipulate both puppets. One of the puppets is the "teacher." The other puppet, the "student," is finding its singing voice. As the "student" puppet begins to sing by echoing the "teacher," encourage the children to applaud, while the "student" puppet "takes a bow." Randomly place the "student" puppet on the hands of willing children, and let them take turns singing for the puppet. It's an uninhibited way to nurture the development of independent singing voices. The children don't perceive that they are singing alone in front of an audience – the puppet is!

HULA HOOPS

• Very young children can perform large-muscle, coordination activities with five large, over-sized hula hoops placed on the floor. Assign 3-4 children to one hula-hoop. While music is playing, instruct children to perform the following:

1) Walk, jog, hop, jump, gallop, tip-toe, stomp, crawl, walk on heels, walk pigeon-toed, walk with toes out, bear walk, fly, swim, and row around the hula hoop.
2) Repeat, but reverse the direction and/or have children move in reverse.
3) Move with one foot inside and one foot outside the hula hoop.
4) Jump into center, and back out.
5) Move with one hand and one foot inside and the other hand and foot outside.
6) Move with two hands inside and two feet outside.
7) All children wearing a designated color hop inside and do a motion.
8) At your command, "Scatter," children go to a new hula hoop.

• Place three over-sized hula hoops on the floor for categorizing rhythm band instruments. Place instruments (at least one for each child) inside the hula hoops accordingly:

1) Instruments which are struck with the hands
2) Instruments which are struck with mallets
3) Instruments which are shaken

Children walk around all three hula hoops to the beat of music. When the music stops, all take an instrument. When the music resumes, all play the instrument to the beat of the music. When the music stops again, each instrument is replaced in the original hula hoop and a new instrument is selected. Continue in this fashion three or four more times, so that children have a chance to play a variety of instruments.

BOXES AND MORE

• While preparing young children for a performance, keep a gift box handy. On colorful cards, print the titles of the songs that the children are learning. When a song is learned, let a child put that card into the gift box. When the last song is learned and its card is placed in the box, decorate the box with ribbon and a bow. At the performance, place the wrapped gift box in a highly visible place, such as on top of the piano. It is a visual reminder for children to take pride in their performance. Their songs are the best gift ever - the "gift of themselves."

• Cover a large, tissue box with contact paper and decorate with musical motifs. Label it: THE MUSIC BOX. Keep it handy for collecting student suggestions, extra credit bonus answers, raffle tickets, and more.

• Use stackable, plastic, labeled "tubbies" for storing and organizing just about anything, including papers, instruments, student folders, song props, equipment and more.

SEE FOR YOURSELF

A mirror mounted on the music room wall for student use is indispensable when practicing singing techniques, motions and choreography. Mirrors tell the truth.

BURIED TREASURE

Children love a treasure hunt. Rig the music classroom ahead of time for a "Surprise Day." Hide stickers, or small, individually wrapped candies in various places within the room. Include such places as the inside of the piano bench, and the top drawer of teacher's desk. (For extra silliness, hide one in the rolled-up cuff of your shirt sleeve.) Make "clue cards" that tell where to look for a hidden surprise. A "clue card" might read: LOOK FOR A SURPRISE ON THE CHALKBOARD LEDGE. Play music games, such as "Name That Tune" (students identify mystery melodies played on piano, recorder or hummed), or "Music Brain Drain" (students answer music course content questions, or demonstrate musical skills). A correct answer wins a "clue card" which leads the student to the hidden treasure.

Note: This game is a great evaluation tool to assess whole-group mastery of musical concepts in a fun, non-threatening way.

SCOPE AND SEQUENCE

Children of all ages benefit from visual aids that describe the scope and sequence of music. Children can construct a "music video" which visually traces the sequence of a song's events as it is manipulated. Songs that tell a story, or ones with many add-on verses such as *This Old Man*, are good choices for videos:

1) Children design each "frame" of the video using single sheets of paper, each depicting a certain scene in the song.
2) Children collate the sheets into correct sequence.
3) Tape the "frames" together so they form one, continuous paper roll.
4) Attach dowel rods at both ends of roll.
5) Insert the scroll into a cardboard box into which a rectangle is cut for the "screen."
6) Record children singing the entire song.
7) Children listen to the tape as they watch their video (by rolling the scroll from the bottom onto the top dowel). Children see as well as hear the way music exists through time.

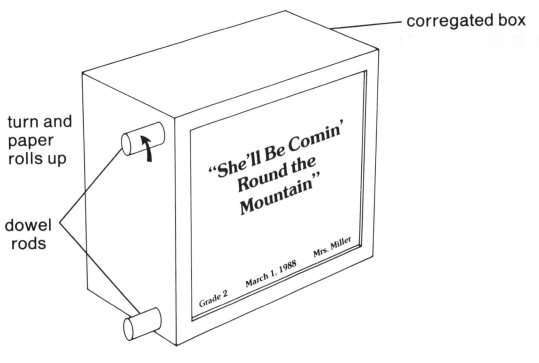

turn and
paper
rolls up

corregated box

dowel
rods

"She'll Be Comin'
Round the
Mountain"

Grade 2   March 1, 1988   Mrs. Miller

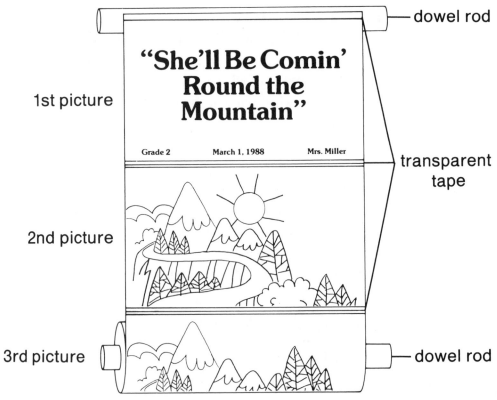

1st picture

2nd picture

3rd picture

"She'll Be Comin'
Round the
Mountain"

Grade 2   March 1, 1988   Mrs. Miller

dowel rod

transparent
tape

dowel rod

TEACHABLE
TACTICS

MAY I HAVE THIS DANCE?

Certain folk dances specify male/female partners, and oftentimes a class includes more girls than boys, or vice versa. Many children become uncomfortable when asked to assume the role of the opposite gender for a dance. Instead of boy/girl partners, label them: red/blue partners, or use names of favorite "non-gender" cartoon characters.

> ▶ **"Instead of boy/girl partners, label them: red/blue partners, or use names of favorite 'non-gender' cartoon characters."**

ONE FOR ALL AND ALL FOR ONE

Establish the Junior (lower elementary) and Senior (upper elementary) Listening Leagues. Each music class within the Listening League becomes familiar with selected pieces of music. Hold a listening contest, in which a predetermined number of points must be accumulated by the classes in each League in order to earn a reward for everyone (perhaps viewing a favorite video during the next music lesson). If the goal is met, every member in the League is a winner; if the League is unable to meet its goal, no one has lost, honorable mention can be made for the effort of each class, and the Leagues can be reorganized for next semester.

NO WHINING ALLOWED!

If there is a disappointment, (for example, "time's up" during a favorite activity), dramatize the mood by humoring your students' moans and groans. On the piano, play the first four measures of *Dolly's Funeral* by Peter Tchaikovsky, or conduct the students through a ten-second "moan and groan" sound effect. When you conduct the cut-off, the sour mood is over.

ATTENTION, PLEASE!

Students appear to be not listening to your instructions? Continue to speak with normal eye contact and hand gestures, but very gradually decrease the volume of your voice until it's barely audible. When students look at you to see "what's wrong," they usually inform you that they cannot hear. Respond with: "Perhaps you were hearing me, but, were you really listening?" Students' attention is once again focused on you.

• Students have difficulty remembering your instructions? Tell students the number of instructions you are about to recite. Number them as you recite them, emphasizing key words. Recite a second time, but omit the key words, allowing students to "fill in the blanks."

• Challenge students to move from one position to another by setting a time limit, like this: "You must be 'frozen' in your new position by the time I sing to the Number 5." Sing up the scale, using numbers. Or, "You must be 'frozen' in your new position by the time the piano music is finished."

Note: Very young children may be asked to "Go to the new space first with your eyes. Now, move to the new space with your body as I sing to the Number 5. You must plant your roots firmly into the ground and be still before I get to 5."

• The entire class is self-absorbed in an activity, and you need to get the attention of the whole group. What is a music teacher to do, without abusing the voice by shouting, or blowing a referee's shrill whistle, neither of which models musical taste. At the start of the school year, establish and practice this signal, nicknamed "the quiet cadence." Use as needed:

Teacher claps, or strikes a drum: ♩ ♫♩ ♩ ♩

Students clap: 𝄽 ♩ ♩ 𝄽

• With young children, sing as many instructions to them as possible, using combinations of pitches and intervals, or improvising with traditional songs. Have them echo-sing the instructions back to you.

MUSICAL CHAIRS

• Upper elementary students seated in rows of chairs/desks in the music room can be challenged to arrange themselves without teacher's help. At the start of the school year, seat students alphabetically. On the second or third music day, tell students that when music starts to play, they must re-alphabetize themselves within their row, before the music stops. Congratulate or award the fastest rows.

• Here's a nifty way to create flexible seating charts. When students are appropriately arranged, transfer the seating arrangement onto a sheet of paper with little "sticky notes." Cut the smallest-size "sticky note" in half, print the student's name on it, and arrange it on the sheet in the order he/she sits. "Sticky notes" are placed in rows on the sheet of paper, in the exact order that students are seated in the classroom. Insert the page into a clear, plastic page protector, and the page of "sticky notes" is intact. When the time comes to change the seating chart, simply lift off the "sticky notes" from the page, and rearrange.

A VERY SPECIAL AWARD

Specify a unique assignment, or extra credit bonus project which could deserve the CREATE Award. This should be one of the highest honors bestowed upon a music student. Students who achieve this award demonstrate:

C uriosity
R esearch
E nthusiasm
A ction
T hought
E nergy

THE GREEN ROOM

Anxious performers are corralled into a waiting area before "show time." Conduct a "tension-lifting" sing-a-long with favorite camp-style songs, or other catchy, nonsense songs. Older students can be easily calmed with a session of "brain teasers," or "mystery" problems which require a question/answer format to solve. Check your local library for sources.

THE JURY'S DECISION, PLEASE

When evaluating a whole-class effort at a particular skill, use the "thumbs up, thumbs down" method. If the effort is judged satisfactory to excellent, show "thumbs up" while calling out: "Bravo!" For an effort that invites repeated practice, show "thumbs down" while calling out: "Baloney! Should we let ourselves get away with that one?"

RULES MEANT TO BE BROKEN

• When students move in a line formation about the music room to the beat of recorded music, allow them to occasionally move the line into the hallway and back. Remember: "You must move quietly in the hall, so that you can still hear the music's beat coming from the music room." This tactic challenges students to refine their listening skills while taking their movements into the hallway, which is usually forbidden territory.

• Occasionally, for the fun and camaraderie of it, allow students to leave their places and join you at the piano or stereo for a "sing-along" of the current songs they are learning. Students can casually gather around the piano with selected soloists seated on the piano bench with you. Students are motivated to sing solos or duets, when they can "sit in the seat of honor."

ANYTHING FOR APPLAUSE

This is pure silliness, children love it, and...it only works once. To illustrate tempo, lead the children in a steady hand clap at a very slow speed. Very gradually, increase the tempo. When the clapping becomes so fast that it runs together and sounds like applause, take a bow and say, "Why thank you. You've been a WONDERFUL audience!"

THE MAGIC WORD

Model common courtesy, manners, and etiquette when handing out instruments or other classroom materials. Keep the item in your hand until the student says, "Thank you." As he/she takes the item from your hand, offer, "You're welcome." It usually doesn't take long for a "grabby" student to realize that you're not going to let go of the item, until he/she remembers the "magic word."

QUIT COMPLAINING!

It's human nature to complain about the weather. When students get the "weather grumpies" sing these songs to lift their spirits:

1) To cure the "cold weather doldrums," sing *In the Good Old Summertime*.

2) To cool off the "hot weather droopies," sing *Frosty the Snowman*.

3) To lift the "rainy day blues," sing *You Are My Sunshine*.

NICKNAMES

When dividing the class into small groups, allow students to give an identity to the group by naming it after TV/movie heroes, fairy tale characters, animals, pizza ingredients, seasonal characters such as elves, reindeer, snowflakes, etc. For example, five cooperative learning groups could be titled: 1) the pepperonis 2) the hams 3) the sausages 4) the anchovies 5) the green peppers.

IT'S ALL IN THE
WAY YOU SAY IT

A NOTEWORTHY ACCOMPLISHMENT

One way of getting students to draw noteheads on the correct line or spaces of the music staff is to word instructions in this manner: "Draw your notehead IN a space, or AROUND a line."

> **"Choose words that invite, rather than demand participation."**

PRETTY PLEASE

Choose words that invite, rather than demand participation, such as:

"Amana, may I please borrow your name for this activity?"
"Diana, may I please borrow you for this game?"
"I'm in need of a friend to help me teach the next motion."
"Who would like to be the 'star' of today's lesson?"

ARE WE HAVING FUN YET?

Instead of referring to student music pages as "work sheets," try calling them "practice pages," "fun sheets," "doodle notes," or "sound ideas." Think of more suggestions that could change children's perceptions of work or effort into fun.

MY VERY OWN INSTRUMENT

Always refer to the singing voice as an instrument. "What are the ways in which it produces the best sound? What are the ways that we take care of it? In what ways could the voice be abused?" Expect only the very best sound that children's voices are capable of producing no matter if they're learning a new song, or putting finishing touches on a performance.

A THINK TANK

Instead of just telling students what to do, offer them thinking questions or statements. For example, rather than: "Please turn to page 38," say: "Please turn to five pages before page 43." Or, rather than: "Please move to the music by stepping the beat and clapping your hands," say: "Please move to the music by moving three body parts." (Be prepared for some creative, clever and simply outlandish interpretations of that statement, such as walking on one foot and two arms; two knees and one elbow, etc.!)

VARIATIONS
ON A THEME

SLIGHT OF HAND

Clapping to the beat of music gets boring if it's always done the same way. Encourage students to vary their style of clapping like this:

Soprano clap: Two fingers tap palm of opposite hand to produce a high-pitched, soft sound.
Alto clap: Four fingers tap palm of opposite hand to produce a medium-high-pitched, slightly-louder sound.
Tenor clap: The usual clap, in which entire palms of both hands smack together to produce a medium-pitched, crisp sound.
Bass clap: Cup hands slightly while smacking both hands together to produce the lowest-pitched, resonant sound.

Lead students to discover that the concept of *dynamics* (loud and soft) is relative to the actual sounds being produced. The bass clap described above sounds at a *forte* (loud) dynamic level when compared to the *piano* (soft) sound produced by the soprano clap. However, the same bass clap is sounding at a mere *piano* dynamic level in relation to that of a sound produced by a bass drum.

A DIFFERENT DUET

There's more than one way to play a piano. Remove the lower front panel from a spinet, console or upright piano. Invite one student to strum the strings while another holds down the damper pedal. Students love the effect. Probe their sound discovery: "Can you tell which are the bass strings? the treble strings? Some of the strings are thick and copper-colored, while some are thin and silver."

INSTRUMENTALLY SPEAKING

Pitched bars on melody instruments don't have to be identified as C, D, E, F, G, A and B. Try giving them these labels, and note how much more fun students seem to have playing the very same instruments they've been playing all along:

C herries
D onuts
E ggs
F rench fries
G rapes
A pples
B ananas

NOW YOU SEE IT, NOW YOU DON'T

Post several cards on which the word "rhythm" is written, in highly visible places within the music room. Throughout the music lesson, each time you mention the word "rhythm" take down the cards one at a time until all have been removed. At the end of the lesson, tell students that the word "rhythm" is still in the music room, only that now it is visible only in their minds. Pass out slips of paper and pencils and have students spell "rhythm" for an extra credit. Never before has the word "rhythm" had so many variations on its spelling.

IT'S ALIVE!

Bring rhythm patterns to life with students forming the notes themselves. The pattern: ♩ ♩ ♫♩ can be created with five students. Two students stand side by side; the third and fourth students stand side by side, and put arms on each other's shoulders (connecting); the fifth student stands alone.

WHAT'S IN A NAME?

Personalize favorite songs by inserting children's names. For example, the traditional song, BINGO, could be adapted this way:

There was a teacher had a child, and Timmy was his name-o.

T - I - M-M-Y, T - I - M-M-Y, T - I - M-M-Y, *and Timmy was his name-o.*

S-A-L- L-I- E, S-A-L- L-I- E, S- A-L- L-I- E, *and Sallie was her name-o.*

KEEPING SCORE

In addition to defining duration and pitch, music notes can serve another function: keeping game scores. Keep score to any game like this: o = four points; ♩. = three points; ♩ = two points; ♩ = one point.

COFFEE, ANYONE?

A popcorn party is a favorite and economical reward. Purchase inexpensive, generic, fluted coffee filters to use as bowls. When each student is all finished, he/she can pick up the crumbs, put in coffee filter, crumple and toss in the trash.

T I N   E A R
TUNE-UP TIME

• Did you hear about the music teacher who asked the out-of-tune singer to "just mouth the words," so that she wouldn't be heard and ruin the musical quality of the rest of the group? The girl grew up and now she says, "I can't sing. When I was little, my music teacher told me to keep quiet." In-tune singing is a skill that is acquired with lots of practice, working the "inner ear" harder than the voice. Some of these games and techniques can be used to encourage accurate intonation while avoiding the possibility of damaging singers' self-concepts.

> **"'I can't sing. When I was little, my music teacher told me to keep quiet.'"**

1) In a large group setting, position the child between and in front of, in-tune singers.
2) When dealing one on one, establish eye contact, and have the child:
   a) Echo these kinds of sounds: howling wind, animal sounds that vary in pitch from high to low like a coyote, or sirens.
   b) Mimic the sound of a slide whistle.
   c) Cover one ear and mouth while singing (the sound appears to be louder inside the head).
   d) Sing with fingers in the ears (inside hearing is even louder).
   e) Imagine to be singing notes which are basketballs going through the net (aiming for head voice).
   f) Sing while placing a hand on top of the head, and aiming the sensation of singing to that spot.
   g) Imagine the bull's eye of a target, and aim first with the ear, then with the voice, before attempting to sing.
   h) Place a vibrating tuning fork near the side of the head, and hum along with the pitch.

• Tune-up before singing a song by playing with some "knock-knock" jokes. Sing the jokes improvising combinations pitches which define the tonal setting of the song, such as *sol-mi-do*. Here are some starters:

Teacher: *Knock knock.* Students: *Who's there?* Teacher: *Mike.* Students: *Mike who?* Teacher: *Microphone.*

Teacher: *Knock knock.* Students: *Who's there?* Teacher: *Jim.* Students: *Jim who?* Teacher: *Gymnasium.*

Teacher: *Knock knock.* Students: *Who's there?* Teacher: *Meg.* Students: *Meg who?* Teacher: *Megaphone.*

TAKING TURNS

• What to do when small children have a difficult time taking turns? Make a game of taking turns. Children form a circle, with a child as the "spinner" in the center. The child closes his/her eyes or wears a blindfold. Play a series of ascending diminished chords in "tremolo" fashion at the piano. While the music plays, the spinning child turns around, one arm extended forward, with the "pointer finger" out. End the music on a major chord, and the spinning child stops, while "freezing" in the pointing stance. The child being pointed at takes the next turn.

• Another way to help small children understand the concept of taking turns: Children make a circle formation and pass a bean bag, ball or stuffed animal from child to child, in one direction, to the beat of a simple song or chant, "This one, that one, let's pick just one. You are it." The child holding the object at the end of the chant takes the next turn.

M O V E M E N T
AND DIRECTION

NAVIGATORS

Obtain a compass, and allow students to determine the North, South, East, and West walls of the music room. Have students create four colorful posters:

1) North, pictured as an icy igloo nestled in a snowbank.
2) South, pictured as a tropical scene with brilliant sun, sandy beach, frothy waves and palm trees.
3) East, pictured as a bright, yellow sun peering out above the horizon.
4) West, pictured as a red sun setting into the horizon.

Place these posters high on the appropriate walls of the music room that correspond with the same direction. Instead of instructing students to "face the wall with the windows," tell them to "face east," and so on.

Note: For broader geographic reinforcement:

1) Ask students to face west while standing in the music room. Ask: "What can you see?" The response might be: "The clock, the chalkboard, the thermostat," etc.
2) Now, ask them to face west while standing in the music room, visualizing the location of that room within the city. Ask: "What can you see now?" The response might be: "The west parking lot, the bus barn, the field," etc.
3) Now, ask them to face west while standing in the music room in the city of their school, visualizing the location of that city within the country. Ask: "What can you see now?" The response might be: (if for example, the school is located in Milwaukee, Wisconsin) "Minnesota, South Dakota, Iowa, Wyoming, Oregon," etc.
4) Now, ask them to face west while standing in the music room in the city of (Milwaukee) which is in the country of The United States, visualizing the location of that country within the world. Ask: "What can you see now?" The response might be: "The Pacific Ocean, Japan, the continent of Asia," etc.

RIGHT AND LEFT

• Students confused about which direction to move in? Students in a circle formation can imagine themselves standing on the face of a large, circular clock. A command of "CW!" instructs students to move in the clockwise direction of the clock's hands; a command of "CCW" instructs them to move in a counter-clockwise direction.

• More about right and left. When a student is instructed to move, for example, the left leg, and inadvertently moves the right leg, maintain a sense of humor while saving him/her from embarrassment by quipping: "That dance step was exactly right! Now, do it with your other left leg!"

• Still more about right and left. Students experiencing difficulty with right and left (or grown-ups, too, for that matter), benefit from the use of stretchy, ankle bands. Choose brightly colored, wide elastic and cut into ankle-sized pieces. Stitch ends together. (Parent volunteers are often eager to help with sewing.) Students and teacher wear the band on the left ankle. When the instructions call for movement to the right or left, the direction is immediately apparent. Over time, remove the bands, in this order: first, the students', then at a later date, the teacher's.

• Honest, only one more thing about right and left. Small children learning to differentiate between right and left hands delight when a sticker is placed on the back of the left hand. Show them how the hand with the sticker can form the letter "L" (for left) when the hand is held up, palm facing away, so that the four fingers are closed together and the thumb is extended away from the fingers.

6 HELLO AND GOODBYE

PERSONALIZING YOUR MUSIC CLASS

Here are two opportunities naturally packed with teachable moments. Make each minute count by using these occasions to reinforce specific musical concepts. By varying the way music class begins and ends, you are stamping the personal signature of your own, unique teaching style on each music lesson.

RINGING IN THE NEW YEAR

RE-MEMBER?

A poster of favorite photos from last year's music classes/performances that show children having fun making music can be most inviting when posted at the door on the very first day of this year's music class.

TV STARS

At an opportune time during the first two weeks of music class, show portions of a video taken from last year's musical performances, which include this year's music students.

A MUSICAL HELLO

HELLO FROM MANY LANDS

Sing a favorite "Hello" song several times, while viewing a world map or globe. Sing the "hello" in various languages. Students can point to the country from which each greeting originates. Here are some starters:

"Hello" in **French**: *"Bonjour." (pronounced: bohn- ZHOOR)*
"Hello" in **German**: *"Guten Morgen." (pronounced: GOOT-en MORG-en)*
"Hello" in **Spanish**: *"Hola" (pronounced: OH-lah)*
"Hello" in **Italian**: *"Buon giorno" (pronounced: boo-OHn jee-OHr-noh)*

A LYRIC TRANSPLANT

Encourage children to improvise new lyrics to a favorite song of greeting. For example, *The More We Get Together* can be adapted:

"The more we sing together...clap together...sway together...laugh together...bark together," etc.

The More We Get Together

GOOD TIMING

Greet music students with a timely song that encourages awareness of current affairs, seasons or special local events. Children won't have to be asked to join in – the spirit of fun will draw them right in. Consider singing:

Take Me Out to the Ball Game on opening day of baseball season.
Fly Me to the Moon on the day of a space launch.
Happy Birthday on the birthday anniversary of a great composer.
The Star Spangled Banner on election day.
Consider Yourself on the opening day of the local high school's performance of "Oliver."

Brainstorm other catchy possibilities.

HALLWAY SHENANIGANS

SILENT SIGNALS

While children are in the hallway about to enter the music room, introduce a specific concept, such as a new rhythm pattern. Ask them to memorize it. Designate a signal, like pulling your ear or scratching your head. Tell the children that at any time during the course of the music lesson, when they see the signal, they may jump up and clap/recite the newly-learned rhythm pattern. Reward the fastest students. Do it several times. It's a silly yet effective way to command children's attention from the very first moment of the music lesson and throughout, while reinforcing the learning of a new concept.

MUSICAL PASSWORD

On another day, in the hallway, prior to the music lesson, hum a melody clue, or clap a rhythm clue to a song or piece of music taught in the previous music lesson. Students must identify the music as their "password" in order to enter the classroom.

PREMIERE PERFORMANCE

Teach a new rhythm or melody pattern in the hallway before entering the music room. Place a drum or set of bells on a table just inside the door. As children enter, each takes a turn to perform the newly-learned pattern before going to his/her place.

S U R P R I S E !

MUSICAL INTRUDER

Prior to the music lesson, hide a ticking metronome in the classroom so it's within audible range. Don't mention it at the start of the lesson - just begin

> "Make it a common practice to surprise students often."

teaching. Let the children gaze around the room in search of the ticking sound, until such time that their curiosity gets the best of them, or it becomes an unbearable intrusion. Ask students to guess where it is and what it is. Allow one child to search for the source of the ticking sound. Once the metronome is found, use it as a visual/aural aid to demonstrate the concepts of tempo and auditory discrimination. Make it a common practice to surprise students often.

BEARING GIFTS

Prior to the music lesson, place a gift-wrapped box containing a prop for a song, in a highly visible place within the room, so that immediately upon entering, students spot the gift. When they inquire as to whom the gift belongs, tell them it's for them from you, and that they may have it during the lesson. Select a student to open the gift. The prop might be a new classroom puppet that "teaches" a new song, or a wind-up music box to demonstrate tempo, or a tuning fork to reinforce a lesson on sound production, etc.

FOLLOW THE
LEADER

FUNNY FEET

For very young children, invite them to "follow the funny feet in front of you" when entering the room, or, when making a large circle formation. This way, children focus on following the footsteps of the child directly ahead, rather than becoming overwhelmed by watching the movements of the entire group.

HAND JIVES

While the music is playing, perform a hand jive as you lead children into the room. Invite them to join in with the jive while they step to the beat of the music. When everyone catches on, change the jive. For example, a favorite hand jive that accompanies music in a *meter in four*:

a) Slap legs.
b) Clap hands.
c) Snap right-hand fingers.
d) Snap left-hand fingers.

Note hand jives in other meters on page 53.

BODY JIVES

For very young children, follow the same activity described above, but instead of hand jives, perform gross motor movements. For example, lead the children in marching, jumping, hopping on one foot, skipping, flying, rowing, jogging, tip-toeing, and more, to the beat of music. Allow them to improvise their own motions.

CATCH!

When teaching the simplest melodic sequences to young children, surprise them at the beginning of the lesson with a bean bag or stuffed animal. While tossing the bean bag to a student to catch, sing "Hello, Laura" on the *sol-mi* (high-low) pitches of the major scale. This child in turn tosses the bean bag to another friend, and sings "hello," and so on. Children may need to sing along with your voice as a guide. Have a picture which shows *high* and *low* visible during this activity. (For example, a picture that shows an airplane and a car, or, a bird and a fish.) During subsequent lessons, gradually include more pitches, *sol-mi-la-re-do*, and different combinations.

> ▶ *"When teaching the simplest melodic sequences to young children, surprise them at the beginning of the lesson with a bean bag or stuffed animal."*

A MUSICAL
GOOD-BYE

GOOD-BYE FROM MANY LANDS

Sing a favorite "Good-bye" song, while viewing a world map or globe.

Sing the "good-bye" in various languages. Students can point to the country from which the language originates. Here are some starters:

"Good-bye" in **French**: *"Au revoir."* (pronounced: oh ruh-VWAHR)
"Good-bye" in **German**: *"Auf Wiedersehen!"* (pronounced: owf VEED-uh-zayen)
"Good-bye" in **Spanish**: *"Adios."* (pronounced: ah-DYOHS)
"Good-bye" in **Italian**: *"Arrivederci."* (pronounced: ahr-ree-veh-dAYr-chee)

LYRIC TRANSPLANT

Encourage young children to improvise new "good-bye" lyrics to a favorite, traditional song. *Skip to My Lou* could be adapted:

"Hop, hop, hop to the door... Fly, fly, fly to the door... Clap, clap, clap to the door... Twirl, twirl, twirl to the door," etc.

SELF-HELP SKILLS

Adapt lyrics about children's self-help skills to the traditional song, *If You're Happy and You Know It*. As each improvised verse is sung, children take turns to line-up at the door. For example:

"If you made your bed today, line right up... If you picked up your toys last night, line right up... If you brushed your teeth today... If you set the table last night... If you combed your hair today. If you hugged your mom today," etc.

Choose other traditional songs that may be your students' favorites.

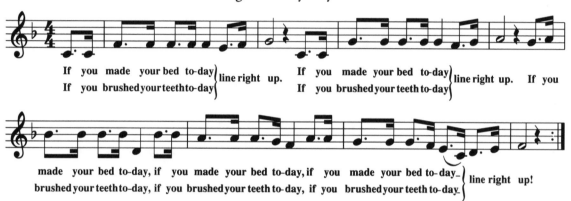

S T E A L I N G
MORE TIME

QUIET ECHOES

If impatient music students are lined-up and waiting for the classroom teacher to arrive, play a rhythm echo game, using body/voice rhythms:

"Here I am, you can see, do what I do after me."

Perform a series of four-beat rhythms, and have students echo. Include clapping, snapping, pointing, patting, jumping, hopping, sneezing, flapping, hissing, snorting, grunting, and other sound effects, but – save this one to quiet everyone down, and bring closure to the activity: Teacher puts index finger to the lips and makes a "shhhh" sound (the universal sound for "be quiet") with this rhythm:

During subsequent lessons, allow a student to lead the activity.

FRONT AND CENTER

When the music lesson is completed, and you're "stuck with time to kill" turn these minutes into learning time, with this favorite activity:

Students are told that they are musical experts. While lined-up, the teacher announces any student's initials. The student with those initials moves about six inches to the side, away from the line. Present the "expert" with a musical problem, such as: Name That Tune (hum a melody), echo clap a rhythm pattern, Name That Term (show a music symbol), or other music content questions. A correct answer wins a place at the front of the line; an incorrect answer stays. All responses are met with applause, correct or not. The student with an incorrect answer chooses a friend to help solve the musical problem.

TOTAL RECALL

Introduce a new concept such as a rhythm or melody pattern at the beginning of the music lesson. Have students perform and memorize it. Tell them that during "line-up and good-bye," they will be asked to recall and perform the pattern. Place a drum, or set of bells on a table just inside the door. As students exit the room, each takes a turn to perform the newly-learned pattern.

INSTRUMENTS AT HOME

With this game, teach young children identification of rhythm instruments, and the correct place for storing them. Ahead of time, cut out pictures of classroom rhythm instruments from music instrument catalogs. Mount on cards. Put cards in a "secret box" that has a slot on the top into which a hand could fit. Children are seated in a circle, and as music plays, the box is passed from child to child. When the music stops, the child holding the box draws out a card which shows an instrument. Reinforce the instrument's name, and show where its "home" is. Children using that instrument put it away and line-up. Continue in this fashion until all instruments are "at home."

NAME THAT TUNE

Obtain a box and fill it with cards which show each letter of the alphabet. Draw one card and call aloud the letter which is on it. Any student whose first name begins with the selected letter, stands. If more than one student stands, select one. This student has five counts (beats) to announce his/her favorite song. If a song is not named while you whisper "one, two, three, four, five," the student stays in place. Other standing students, whose names also begin with the selected letter, each have five seconds to do likewise. If a song is named, the student then lines up. The letter card is put aside to prevent it from being called again. The game continues in this fashion. The hilarity happens when students hastily name their favorite song. In an attempt to get an answer in "under the wire," students often name the very first song that pops into their minds. Older students have been known to announce favorite songs: *Twinkle, Twinkle Little Star, Are You Sleeping, Where is Thumbkin,* and other "toddler" favorites.

PLACES, EVERYBODY!

• With children facing center in a circle formation, choose three leaders, and place them equi-distant, and in front of three students inside the circle. All recite a favorite chant while the leaders pat the beat into the palms of the hands of each student in turn, going in one direction around the circle. When the chant is over, the three leaders line-up at the door, and the children who received the last pat are the new leaders. Continue in this fashion until only two or three are left. They stand close together in a small circle and clap the chant for the last time. Lined-up children continue to recite the chant throughout the game.

Some favorite chants:

This one, that one, let's pick just one.
YOU are it!

Bumble, bumble, bumble bee
Stung little (name) right in the knee!

In and out, round about
O-U-T and that spells out!

• Children's circle singing games (play party games) lend themselves well to "good-bye" activities. For example, choose three leaders to move to the beat around the outside of a children's circle formation, while all sing the verse to *Rig a Jig Jig*. At the refrain, the three leaders choose three nearby children to perform the hand jive as partners: Partners hold hands and swing arms left and right to the beat. At the conclusion of the song, the original three leaders line-up at the door, and the the chosen children assume the role of the original three leaders. The game continues in this fashion.

7 MUSICAL WARM-UPS

MIND - BODY - VOICE

Why does a runner stretch and loosen muscles before running a race? Why does a football player perform calisthenics and agile running steps before playing football? Why does a piano player play scales and arpeggios before playing a piano recital? Why does a vocalist practice vocalises before singing a vocal performance? All of these individuals "warm-up" the mind, body, hands, or voice so that they can operate at peak efficiency.

> **"When selecting warm-ups, choose activities for children which are bite-sized, meaningful learning experiences that reinforce musical concepts contained in the lesson."**

Children attending vocal music class require a unique kind of warm-up to get their motors running at peak efficiency. Attitude warm-ups, posture warm-ups, motor warm-ups, breathing warm-ups, pitch perception and vocal warm-ups which are brief, repetitive and fun, limber the child's mind, body, and voice, for maximum musical learning.

When selecting warm-ups, choose activities for children which are:

1) Bite-sized, meaningful learning experiences that reinforce musical concepts contained in the lesson, or are excerpts of actual music contained in the music lesson.

2) Age-appropriate and ability-appropriate for individual student groups.

Here are some warm-ups which serve to "limber up" the development of children's behavioral, social, physiological, musical skills. Warm-ups may be as few as one, or as many as three or four per music lesson.

ATTITUDE
WARM-UP

THE WINNING ATTITUDE CHECKLIST

Select a student leader to recite the "Winning Attitude" Checklist. After each check point, students respond: "Check." When the checklist is routinely reviewed at the start of each music lesson, students gradually acquire the habit of perceiving themselves as "winners." Notice how the focus in attitude shifts from the importance of "me" to the importance of "we."

> ▶ **"When the checklist is routinely reviewed at the start of each music lesson, students gradually acquire the habit of perceiving themselves as winners."**

1) I am welcome in music class.
2) Through music, I explore and enjoy my creative self.
3) I am an important member of our music team.
4) Without me, our music is not nearly as beautiful.
5) Together as friends, we are winners at making beautiful music.

A LITTLE PARODY

Very young children can warm-up to the theme of the music lesson by improvising "new" words to "old" songs. For example, instead of singing *The Wheels on the Bus*, children can sing:

1) "The children in our school go read, read, read," etc. (pretend to hold an open book)
2) "The teachers in our school go very very good," etc. (pat self on the shoulder)
3) "The parents in our school go study, study, study," etc. (point a finger to the beat)
4) "The principal in our school goes how are you?" etc. (shake the hand of a nearby child)
5) "The art teacher goes draw, draw, draw," etc. (pretend to sketch)
6) "The gym teacher goes run, run, run," etc. (jog in place)
7) "The computer teacher goes type, type, type," etc. (pretend to type on a keyboard)
8) "The cooks in the school go stir, stir, stir," etc. (pretend to stir)
9) "The Spanish teacher goes hola, hola, hola," etc. (wave hello)
10) "The music teacher goes tra la la," etc. (conduct with two index fingers)

M O T O R
WARM-UPS

THE BEAT JIVE

Create a four-beat (easy) or eight-beat (challenging) sequence of body motions. For example:

1) Slap legs.
2) Clap hands.
3) Snap right fingers.
4) Snap left fingers.

Or add to it:

5) Pat head with both hands.
6) Pat shoulders.
7) Slap palms of hands together (as if crashing cymbals together).
8) Slap palms of hands together in opposite direction of step 7.

Lead students through this sequence of body motions, counting each motion out loud. When fluent, call out numbers in random order to challenge students' memories at recalling the corresponding motions. Then, while listening to music with meter in *two* or *four*, invite students to perform the body jive, repeatedly throughout the duration of the music. The next time students perform this activity, choose music with a different tempo.

For more challenge, call out a number to which the corresponding motion is to be omitted, (for example, "5"). While music plays, students perform the jive, but "rest" on beat 5 instead of patting the head. Gradually, call out additional numbers that are to be omitted, until only one or two motions are left to perform. The trick is to perform the motions at the proper times by keeping a steady beat! Make sure your students are either counting aloud, or silently "in their heads." Allow a student to lead the activity.

Try the same activity with meter in *three* or *six*. Here are some suggestions for the beat jive:

1) Clap hands.
2) Snap fingers of one hand.
3) Snap fingers of the other hand.

Or, add to it:

4) Pat head.
5) Pat shoulders.
6) Pat waist.

Variation: Divide students into two groups. As they perform the body jive to music, sound a tambourine which signals one group to "freeze," while the remaining group continues the motions. At the next tambourine sound, the "freezing" group resumes the beat jive, while the remaining group "freezes." And so on.

BEAT AEROBICS

While high-energy music (such as a march) is playing, lead students in actual aerobic exercise to get the blood flowing. Upper body exercises, or those which bring the arms over the head encourage awareness of keeping the upper body lifted out of the waist when singing. For example:

• Waist Bends
   1) Pat head.
   2) Pat waist.
   3) Pat toes.
   4) Pat waist.
   5) Repeat throughout music.

• Jumping Jacks
   1) Jump into an open-leg stance while arms slap outside of thighs.
   2) Jump into a closed-leg stance while hands clap overhead.
   3) Repeat.

MUSCLES LIKE RUBBER BANDS

Invite students to imagine that the neck, back, shoulders and arms are made of rubber bands. While music is playing, lead students in these motions, starting with eight beats of motions. Proceed to four beats of motions. Then two motions, finally one motion to the beat:

1) Nod head forward.
2) Nod head backward.
3) Nod head to right side.
4) Nod head to left side.
5) Drop left shoulder forward with left hand on hip.
6) Drop left shoulder backward with left hand on him.
7) Repeat Step 5 with right shoulder.
8) Repeat Step 6 with right shoulder
9) Make small forward arm circles with arms extended at the sides.
10) Make small backward arm circles with arms extended at the sides.
11) Bend forward at the waist.
12) Bend backward at the waist.
13) Bend to the right side.
13) Bend to the left side.

WEE FOLKS

Arrange children in a standing circle formation. Choose one to be the "beatnik." From the center of the circle, the beatnik leads the other children in improvised motions to the beat of the song, *Jimmy Crack Corn*. For example:

"Jump up high, and shout hurray,
Jump up high, and shout hurray,
Jump up high, and shout hurray.
We'll have a happy day."

At the conclusion of the verse, the beatnik closes his/her eyes and spins around to piano music with an outstretched arm and "pointer finger." When the music stops, the child stops spinning, opens eyes, and announces the name of the child to whom he/she is pointing. This child is the new beatnik and the activity begins again with a new improvised motion.

Variation: Play the same game using the song *If You're Happy and You Know It*. For example: "If you're happy and you know it, clap your hands, stamp your feet, wiggle your fingers, bend down low, blink your eyes," and more.

P O S T U R E
WARM-UPS

MONKEY SEE, MONKEY DO

Model an appropriate sitting posture for singing:

1) Sit forward on seat of chair, so spine is not touching chair.
2) Place both feet on floor, with one foot slightly ahead of other. The foot in back has toes touching floor, heel up.
3) Imagine the sensation of the upper body being lifted up and out from the abdominal area.
4) With shoulders, head, and neck in a level position, lean the upper body slightly forward. This posture encourages students to experience a sensation of "anticipated forward motion," and helps them to "lean into" their music.

For standing posture, one foot is placed slightly ahead of the other, with body weight balanced over both feet. Steps 3 and 4 are the same.

JACK-IN-THE-BOX?

▶ "Encourage singers to imagine that the tops of their heads are touching the ceiling of the music room."

Once correct sitting posture is assumed, play this silly, little game. At any time during the lesson, call out: "Stand Up!" Students who are indeed sitting forward in their chairs are the first ones to pop up onto their feet. The first one to pop up is rewarded with a sticker, stamp or other small, positive reinforcement. Then, tell students to resume sitting. Play again at ANY time throughout the entire music lesson. This tactic encourages awareness of correct singing posture while it always manages to "keep kids on their toes!"

SITTING UP

Encourage singers to imagine that the tops of their heads are "touching the ceiling of the music room," or that "a flexible wire which comes down from the ceiling inserts through their skulls and down through their spines and into the seats of their chairs." This mental imagery encourages effort at maintaining an appropriate, upright sitting posture.

B R E A T H I N G
W A R M - U P S

FLOATING LIKE A FEATHER

Describe to singers the way in which the breath acts as the "actuator" in producing a vocal sound: "The pressure of the breath against the vocal cords causes them to vibrate, and produce sound." The amount of air, and the rate at which the air flows against the vocal cords, among other factors, help determine the *duration* and *volume* of the vocal sound. Tell singers to imagine how a sung musical tone is like a feather. Show the way a feather floats in the air:

1) Holding the feather close to your mouth, aim it in an upward direction, and send the feather on its way with a whoosh of air.
2) Do this several times, each time altering the exhalation of breath:
   a) short burst of air
   b) long stream of air
   c) gentle whisk of air
   d) full-forced blast of air.
3) Try combinations: a gentle, short burst of air, or a full-forced, short burst of air, or a gentle, long stream of air, and a full-forced long stream of air. What happens to the movement of the feather?
4) Encourage students to experiment with the volume and duration of their vocal tones, by changing the amount and speed of their airflow against their vocal cords. While singing the syllable "loo" on A above middle C, ask them to change their airflow in the same manner as described in step 2. What happens to the quality of the vocal tone?
5) Allow students to discover the connection between the amount and speed of airflow against the vocal chords, and the resultant vocal sound. They should discover that a short burst of air against the vocal cords results in a vocal tone of short duration, and a long stream of air results in a vocal tone of longer duration. A gentle airflow against the vocal cords results in a softer vocal tone. Conversely, a full-forced airflow results in a louder vocal tone.

This technique can be applied to a balloon. By inviting children to blow into their own balloons, they can determine for themselves the relationship between differing amounts and rates of airflow and changes in size of the balloon.

Ask children to watch wind chimes in the breeze. Imagine the wind chimes to be the human vocal cords. How does the breeze affect the sound that is produced?

THE "B.B.B."

The Big Belly Breath is an exercise which dramatizes for children the actual breathing process which occurs before and during phonation (tonal attack):

1) With arms lowered at the sides, very slowly raise them outward to the sides, and upward, while inhaling very slowly and inaudibly ("filling up with air"), as if to allow air to fill up the waist, chest, throat and head.

2) When the hands touch one another above the head, very slowly bring arms back down, keeping the rib cage lifted, while at the same time exhaling on a "whooooo" (whisper soft) sound.

3) When the arms are back down at the sides, and all air is just about expelled, make a long "shhhhhh" sound, or a hard "ck" sound, expelling the remaining air. Pronouncing either one of these two consonant blends at the end of the airflow causes the breathing muscles below the rib cage to noticeably activate. Says one child: "It feels like my belly button touches my backbone."

▶ **"When singers are about to perform, and nervous or anxious feelings become overwhelming, conduct them two times through the 'B.B.B.'"**

4) Each time singers do the "B.B.B.," count softly to measure the duration of airflow. With each practice, encourage singers to aim for increased control over the rate of exhalation.

5) Once the "B.B.B." is learned, it can be routinely practiced, and then only alluded to when inhaling before singing actual phrases of song. Remember, the "B.B.B." is an elongated version of the actual breathing process. Before and during the act of singing, breathing is an almost instantaneous process, just like it is before speaking.

Note: When singers are about to perform, and nervous or anxious feelings become overwhelming, conduct them two times through the "B.B.B." The exercise helps slow down accelerated heart rates, and fast-paced singing tendencies, while providing a calming, soothing relief for the "heebie jeebies," "willie nillies," or "mully grums" (children's terms for the "butterflies which flutter in a nervous stomach").

FILL 'ER UP

Consider describing these graphic images to your singers to help them breathe in a natural, relaxed manner before singing phrases of music. These verbal analogies help children reduce their bodily tensions, especially in the shoulders, back and neck areas, and promote a flexible, yet controlled, vocal demeanor. Invite your singers to:

> **"Let air in from the bottom of the shoes to the top of the head."**

"Naturally assume an instantaneous intake of air."
"Inhale with the feeling of an inside yawn at the back of the throat."
"Let air in from the bottom of the shoes to the top of the head."

JOIN RIGHT IN

• A fun, lively, age-appropriate and contagious song is: *The Happy Wanderer*, by Fred Mueller. It contains lots of built-in, vocal warm-ups:

  1) long vocal phrases (verse)
  2) short vocal phrases (refrain)
  3) legato vocal articulation (verse)
  4) staccato vocal articulation (refrain)
  5) melody moving by step (verse)
  6) melody moving by skips and leaps (refrain)
  7) gradual upward extension of vocal range (refrain)
  8) diaphragmatic breath control with "ha ha ha ha ha ha" (refrain)

• How about a "blues improvisation" for warming up the voice? Listen to *Minnie The Moocher*, recorded by Cab Calloway. Using a call and response format, improvise catchy little melodic phrases using vocal scat syllables, such as: *"doo-bee, doo-wah, scoo-bee, dweet-dweet, 'ndah-dah, bah-dah, nah-nah,"* and more. Sing a blues-style phrase with altered third, fifth or seventh scale tones (blue notes) and invite your singers to echo. The piano or guitar accompanies with easy chords, and/or supplies a rhythmic bass ostinato. Guaranteed giggles and spontaneous singing when this activity is lead by the children themselves!

V O C A L
WARM-UPS

WARM-UPS FOR DEVELOPING VOCAL FOCUS:

• Singers hold the last syllable of the word "crooning," like "nnnng." The jaw remains loose and flexible. Then, while concentrating on a balanced,

▶ *"Sing with smiling eyes on the inside of your head."*

vibrating sensation in the upper head, sinus, pharynx (soft palate) and chest areas, change the vocal sound to "eh." This is sung on *"sol fa mi re do."* Begin the exercise in the low range and continue in an upward direction by half-steps stopping at the comfortable limit of the upper range. This exercise helps singers to sensate their vocal tones in the upper pharynx, and resonate their vocal tones in the resonant areas of the head. For extra ear training challenge, instead of progressing in an upward direction by half-steps, play chords at random, to which the singers can modulate.

1. Nng-eh, nng-eh, nng-eh, nng-eh,   nng-eh,   nng-eh, nng-eh, nng-eh, nng-eh,   nng-eh, etc.
2. Nng-ah, nng-ah, nng-ah, nng-ah,   nng-ah,   nng-ah, nng-ah, nng-ah, nng-ah,   nng-ah, etc.

• Use graphic mental images to describe the sensation of resonant singing tones with a "frontal focus." Focus balanced vibration evenly throughout the head, pharynx, mouth, and sinus areas:

"Sing as if you were blowing out birthday candles with singing tones coming from a yawn at the upper part of the back of your mouth, and out through your eyes."

"Sing as if a bumblebee were buzzing, and tickling the roof at the back of your mouth."

"Sing as if your tones were coming from your eyes and going through a basketball hoop."

"Sing as if your tones were spiraling upward and outward from a yawn at the roof of your mouth and through your eyes."

"Sing with smiling eyes on the inside of your head."

WARM-UPS FOR DEVELOPING VOCAL RANGE

• Singers sing the "ee" vowel sound in a smooth and connected manner on *do re mi fa sol fa mi re do*. Begin the exercise in mid-range and continue in an upward direction by half-steps, keeping the sensation focused in the soft palate. The jaw should be flexible, not rigid. When singers are convinced they have reached the musical stratosphere, or as high as they can comfortably sing, stop. Repeat the exercise, but for the descending five notes, open the vowel sound to "ah."

Note: Adapt the same warm-up to include other open vowel sounds such as these: "scoo-bee-doo-bee-doo-bee-doo-bee-doo," "yah-bah-yah-bah-dah-bah-dah-bah-doo," or "no-way-no-way-no-way-no-way-no."

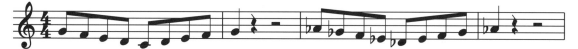

• Take familiar little melodies, such as the melody to *This Old Man* and sing the entire melody on the syllable: "doot." Repeat, a half step higher, and change the syllable to "deet," "hah," "noh," etc. Make sure to include all of the open vowel sounds. Ah, eh, ee, oh, oo. Sing many times, and allow your singers to select the next syllable! Vary the meter, tempo, dynamics, and staccato/legato singing style with each rendition. For fun and silliness, establish a signal, such as a wink of the eye. Each time singers observe your signal, they stop audible singing, and continue inaudible singing. At the signal again, they resume audible singing. This technique helps singers increase their mental alertness!

Note: This idea originated from a student. Any time students are singing, a *fermata* flash card is held up by a selected student. When the card is flashed, the word presently being sung is held, until the teacher cuts it off. Students immediately resume singing.

WARM-UPS FOR DEVELOPING VOCAL DICTION

• Think about the song, *Supercalifragilisticexpialidocious* from the Walt Disney movie, *Mary Poppins*. Children naturally tend to over-emphasize their diction in order to enunciate this nonsense word accurately, and in doing so, achieve correct diction. Also, consider the song *Bibbidi Bobbidi Boo* from the Walt Disney movie, *Cinderella*. It also has nonsense words with alliteration, and plosive consonant sounds which challenge articulation.

• Twist-tonguers, or was that tongue-twisters? Help children articulate words with this tip: Imagine that each word is individually cut from dough with a cookie cutter. The word has "crisp, well-defined edges." Invite singers to join you in a spoken rendition of these favorite little gems. (Chant or sing on a designated pitch(es) many times, gradually increasing the tempo.)

Crock pot.
Unique New York.
Truly rural.
Tweedle Dee, Tweedle Dum.
Greedy green geese.
Preshrunk shirt.
Peggy Babcock.
Double bubble gum bubbles double.
Strange strategic statistics.

• Take the tongue-twister, "Unique New York" (page 133) and set it to a boogie woogie piano accompaniment. Conduct the singing in a "call and response" format.

• These two songs can take on a lyric transplant to become effective diction warm-ups: *Oh Susannah* and *The Battle Hymn of the Republic*. Try either song with these new lyrics:

Four funny little foxes wearing phony feather wigs
Had a picnic in the forest eating frankfurters and figs.
While a cheerful chimp from Charleston sat chatting in a chair
And sixteen chicks did tumbling tricks at Timbuktu Town Fair.

Unique New York

(Diction Warm-up)

By Cheryl Lavender

WARM-UPS FOR DEVELOPING OPEN VOWEL SOUNDS

• Invite singers to sing a known song by singing all consonants inaudibly, and singing all vowels audibly. Encourage them to exaggerate the movement of the lips, teeth, tongue and jaw in order to emphasize the distinct, open vowel sounds. The vowels are highlighted in a fun way! Have your singers sing the song again, only this time include the consonants. Remind singers to focus on the large spatial sensation in the pharynx which was emphasized earlier.

• Ask your singers to silently sing a known song while pretending to be trapped in a soundproof, clear glass closet. Ask another student (to whom the song's title is a mystery) to watch the singers' exaggerated mouth and jaw movements and identify the song's title. Remind singers that exaggerated facial expressions can also help to convey the mood of the song and the meaning of the lyrics.

WARM-UPS FOR DEVELOPING ACCURATE PITCH PERCEPTION

• Begin every singing class by tuning up together with the the pitch A-440. Sound the "A" on the piano, recorder, or pitch pipe. Singers hum or sing the pitch on the syllable "loo." After much practice, play a series of related triads in all inversions while singers hold the "A" pitch :

1) A-major/minor/augmented/diminished chord. Ask singers: "Where is the "A" sounding? Is it the top, middle or bottom tone of the chord?"
2) D-major/minor/diminished chord. Ask singers: "Where is the "A" sounding? Is it the top, middle or bottom tone of the chord?"
3) F-major/augmented chord. Ask singers: "Where is the "A" sounding? Is it the top, middle or bottom tone of the chord?"
4) F-sharp minor/diminished chord. Ask singers: "Where is the "A" sounding? Is it the top, middle or bottom tone of the chord?"
5) C-sharp augmented chord. Ask singers: "Where is the "A" sounding? Is it the top, middle or bottom tone of the chord?"

After much practice hearing the "A" pitch accompanied with related chords, play a series of non-related triads, challenging singers to maintain accurate pitch production while hearing a cacophony of confusing, accompaniment triads!

• Play various examples of harmonic intervals, such as perfect fourths or fifths, major and minor seconds or thirds, tri-tones, etc. Invite students to close their eyes, and mentally discern the number of tones that they are hearing. When they identify the correct number (two distinct tones) play the harmonic interval again, and invite them to hum or sing on "loo" the top pitch, then the bottom pitch. When they are successful, play the interval melodically for reinforcement. Progress to triads and four note chords, in all inversions. Once students sing a designated pitch accurately, play the interval, triad or four-note chord melodically, stressing the designated pitch in relation to the other pitches in the chord.

WARM-UPS FOR DEVELOPING AN INNER EAR FOR HARMONY

• Invite your singers to sing the major scale as a harmony warm-up by progressing through each of the following steps:

1) All singers sing the ascending major scale: *do re mi fa sol la ti do.*
2) All singers sing *do* of the major scale audibly, then sing *re mi fa sol la ti* inaudibly, then audibly on the last *do.* Did they concentrate on "hearing the scale in their inner ears" so that the last *do* sounded "in tune"?
3) One-half of singers sing an ascending major scale, while the other half of singers sing a descending major scale (contrary motion).

4) One-half of singers sing an ascending major scale, plus *re* of the adjacent, next octave before descending the scale, and the other half of singers enter a "third" behind (two pitches later), so that the two groups of singers sing the major exactly a third apart.

1st Group:
Do Re Mi Fa Sol La Ti Do   Re Do Ti La   Sol Fa Mi Re   Do

2nd Group:
Do Re Mi Fa Sol La   Ri Do Re Do Ti La Sol Fa   Mi Re Do

5) Divide singers into three groups and repeat step 3. (When the third group of singers enters, the three singing groups create triadic harmony both up and down the major scale.) Experiment by changing the rhythm, meter, tempo, staccato/legato articulation, volume, and syllables (perhaps "loo" or "nah").

1st Group:
Do Re Mi Fa Sol La Ti Do   Re Do Ti La Sol Fa Mi Re   Do

2nd Group:
Do Re Mi Fa Sol La   Ti Do Re Do Ti La Sol Fa   Mi Re Do

3rd Group:
Do Re Mi Fa   Sol La Ti Do Re Do Ti La   Sol Fa Mi Re Do

6) Having first designated one group to be *sol*, one group to be *mi*, and the remaining group to be low *do*, have the three singing groups sing altogether an ascending scale including *re* of the next octave. As they descend the scale, the *sol* group holds their tone, the *mi* group holds their tone, and the *do* group holds their tone. When all tones have been held in tune, cut off the sound. The result: the tonic triad, formed within the context of the whole scale.

7) Follow step 5, except that, on the descending scale, a designated singing group holds *la*, another group holds *fa*, and the remaining group holds *re*. This sounding triad resolves itself altogether with your signal – *la* resolves to *sol*, *fa* resolves to *mi*, and *re* resolves to *do*.

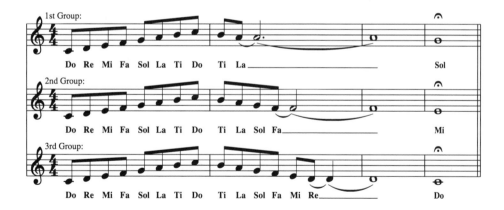

• A simple and effective use of songs having common harmonic progressions and meters is to pair them up as "partner songs." See Partner Songs on page 68 for song suggestions. Give some thought to having the piano be one of the "voices" until the growing harmony settles into your singers' ears.

• Rounds and canons of all kinds are natural learning experiences for creating harmony. Once harmony is achieved, invite singers to sing the round or canon in two different keys, for a poly-tonal effect.

• A three-part chordal harmony can be visually represented with a non-traditional "sound map." Each of three singing groups learns one of these phrases:

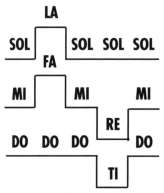

The patterns may be sung on the syllable "loo," or may be adapted to a phrase of words, such as "Merry Christmas," "Viva La Musica" (long live music!), or "Happy Birthday," and more. Make sure singers trade parts in order to experience harmony from more than one angle. Conduct this harmony warm-up by singing it many times, each rendition ascending by half steps.

For example:
SOL ——————————   LA ——————————
Merry, Merry Christmas   Merry Merry Christmas   etc.

8 INTRODUCING & DIGESTING
NEW SONGS
IDEAS THAT REALLY WORK

*"*C*atching flies with honey... Dangling a carrot in front of a horse... Giving candy to a baby..."*

Each of these cliches describes the act of enticing an individual into performing a desired behavior. There is no use of force. An individual is motivated to action, driven by his/her own perceived power of personal choice. It's really just another way of describing a successful "sales pitch." A good salesperson uses techniques which, in the least amount of time, persuade the consumer to want to buy. It's true that "you can lead a horse to water, but you can't force him to drink," however, if the water is located near a bucket of oats, apples and carrots, odds are increased that the horse may want to drink.

> **"Like the salesperson, isn't the educator also playing the role of 'selling' students on the idea of 'wanting to buy into' what is being taught?"**

Isn't it the same with teaching? Like the salesperson, isn't the educator also playing the role of "selling" students on the idea of "wanting to buying into" what is being taught? Below are some techniques that can help "bait" your students' interest when being introduced to new songs, and continue to keep them "hooked" throughout the learning process.

INTRODUCING
NEW SONGS

FAITHFUL SIDEKICKS

• Bring a paper sack, or gift box which contains a surprise prop. The prop can be any object that relates to the theme, style, or musical concept of the new song. Select a student to open the sack or box, and display the prop. Questions generate thinking responses: "What do you think our next song is about?" "What might this have to do with our next song?" Positively reinforce all thinking responses.

• Locate books, pictures and/or illustrations from the library which clarify the time and place of the new song's origin, as well as bring more meaning to the song. For example, when introducing the song, *We Shall Overcome*, a brief history and pictorial describing the life and times of Dr. Martin Luther King, Jr. help to highlight the national holiday.

• Read a short story which reinforces the theme, style or musical concept of a new song. Children of all ages love to be read to, and a story can be just the right element for creating the learning mood for a particular song. Share feelings and thoughts.

I CAN'T BELIEVE I SANG THE WHOLE SONG!

• When teaching students to sing a new song, allow them to hear it first in its entirety. Only after they have experienced the whole of the new song, can they perceive learning its parts as they are extracted and rehearsed. Vary the listening experiences with the new melody: students may hear it sung, performed on song bells, recorder, piano, etc.

> "When teaching students to sing a new song, allow them to hear it first in its entirety. Only after they have experienced the whole of the new song, can they perceive learning its parts."

• Sing a new song for students. Sing again, leaving out ending words of phrases, typically the rhyming words. Invite students to sing the "missing words." Sing again, leaving out even more words. Continue in this fashion, until students are singing the entire song with you.

• Sing a new song for students. Repeat, and invite students to echo one phrase of words at a time. Proceed to two phrases at a time. Progress to whole verses at a time, until entire song is learned.

• A variation on echo-singing: Instead of asking children to echo-sing a phrase of words, invite them to echo-clap the rhythm of a phrase of sung words. Later, discover long and short sounds and their corresponding note values. At another time, help the students understand the concept of "rhythm of the words" by matching up the clapping phrases with flash cards on which the corresponding rhythms are notated.

• Consider not using the piano when introducing new melodies to children. The piano can become a crutch for some children, whose "in-tune" singing skills are being developed.

TRANSFERRING CONCEPTS

• Transfer a previously learned concept(s) to a new song. For example:

1) Hum or play the melody with or without accompaniment, encouraging students to focus their listening skills on a particular concept(s): (rhythm, meter, melody, harmony, form, tempo, dynamics or style).

2) Discover the previously-learned concept in the new song.

3) Recite the text, or words of the song.

4) Share thinking about the meaning of the words.

5) Sing the complete song.

6) Teach students to sing the song.

> **"Ask questions which generate thinking responses, and encourage the use of a musical vocabulary, essential to the building of a student's overall musicianship."**

• Transfer a previously-learned concept by giving students a set of questions to which the answers can be found only by listening with "detective ears" to the new song. For example, some questions might be:

"Do you hear melody moving in mostly upward or downward direction?"
" Do you hear mostly long or short notes?"
"Can you identify the meter?"
"Is the tempo fast, moderate or slow?"
"Does the melody/harmony sound mostly major or minor?"
What words can you use to describe the style?"

Questions like these not only generate thinking responses, but also encourage the use of a musical vocabulary, essential to the building of a student's overall musicianship.

• Play "Private Investigator:"

1) Students listen to the new song for the first time.

2) Next, they are given the notation to follow while listening to it for the second time.

3) Pretending to be "private investigators," students are asked to discover the "puzzle pieces" that when put together, create the whole song. Discover, and transfer these previously-learned concepts:

a) alike and different rhythm patterns

b) alike and different melodic phrases

c) pitches in sequence, pitches in imitation

d) repeated rhythm or melody patterns

e) rhyming words

f) meter

g) harmony

h) form

i) interpretive markings

• Transfer the learned concepts of music notes, rests, symbols and terms to a new song by inviting students to locate and highlight them in the notation. For example:

1) *"Draw a rectangle around the Treble Clef."* (𝄞)

2) *"Draw a circle around the dotted eighth notes."* (♪. ♫)

3) *"Draw a triangle around D.S. al Fine, and, the segno sign (𝄋)."*

4) *"Draw a square around the fermata. (𝄐)."*

T W E N T Y
GUIDELINES
FOR CHOOSING AND INTRODUCING SONGS
TO VERY YOUNG OR SPECIAL-NEEDS CHILDREN

1) Choose songs and singing games which teach:

a) Specific skills, such as taking turns, playing instruments, executing movements, etc. or,

b) Concepts, such as positive self-esteem, feelings, numbers, letters, colors, seasons, etc.

2) Choose songs which are simple in form, rhythmic structure, and melodic range.

3) Choose songs to which movement and drama can be easily added.

4) Choose "verse/refrain" songs that encourage "short term memories" to join in at each familiar refrain.

5) Know the song thoroughly. Rehearse teaching the song ahead of time.

6) Tell a story about the song to set the learning mood, and gain children's attention.

7) Arouse children's interest by having them "mirror" you performing the motions/movements to the new song, minus the words:

a) Choose one child to mirror the motions with you.

b) Invite remaining children to mirror you and the selected child. Encourage thinking responses with the question: "From the motions we just performed, can you tell what the new song might be about?" Positively acknowledge all thinking responses.

8) Whisper the song's theme into a child's ear. Perhaps the song is about an animal, a rainy day, a favorite food, a person, an activity, etc. Invite the child to silently "play act" what the song is about for other children to guess.

9) Invite children to listen as you sing the entire song. Ask questions to encourage attentive listening.

10) Have a puppet sing the song to children. When children are familiar with the song, allow individuals to manipulate the puppet while singing the song. This tactic encourages independent singing while it avoids feelings of "being put on the spot."

11) Model a steady, patting heartbeat and encourage children to mirror the beat during singing. A felt heart, taped to the shirt is an excellent incentive.

12) Following the initial listening experience of a new song, repeat the song, leaving out ending words of phrases (typically the rhyming words). Invite children to sing the missing words. Sing the song again, leaving out more words. Continue, in this fashion until the children are singing the entire song with you.

13) Following the initial listening experience of a new song, invite children to echo each phrase after you. Progress to two phrases at a time, and so on, until the song is learned.

14) It is much easier to invite children to "make beautiful music," rather than tell them to "sing." Allow them to join in naturally. Try not to be disappointed in weak or "out of tune" singing. For some children, this may be their first attempt at making music, and singing thrives when any and all vocal contributions to the song are respected and appreciated by the teacher.

15) Be enthusiastic! Smile often. Singing together with children is great fun! You need not possess a high-calibre singing voice, but must possess the desire to lead children in singing. Shared mistakes and spontaneous laughter bond teacher and child together.

16) Use colorful props which are visually and kinesthetically stimulating to children. Surprise them. Let them guess what you've brought to music class. Keep them curious.

> "A new song is like a new friend. We get to know it better as we play with it each day."

17) Repeat a newly-learned song on many consecutive days. Very young children thrive on repetition. Repetition and routine breed security. A new song is like a new friend: "We get to know it better as we play with it each day."

18) During a singing game, if children make suggestions, try them. Then, the singing game becomes the children's game, not the teacher's game.

19) During a singing game, try to give every child a turn. This is paramount when nurturing a child's self-concept.

20) Touch children often, in a manner of encouragement and affection. A touch can say, "You are a valuable person to me." The bond of music-making is a marvelous gift for grown-up and child alike.

DIGESTING NEW SONGS

BEAT VS. RHYTHM

• After a new melody is learned, challenge singers to differentiate between the song's beat and rhythm:

1) Entire group performs the song by clapping the rhythm of the words (words are sung inaudibly).

2) Entire group sings the song and taps the beat with the foot.

3) Entire group thinks the song and taps the beat with the foot while clapping the rhythm of the words (words sung inaudibly).

4) Repeat step two, but, at your signal (perhaps a ring on triangle), students just tap the beat with foot; at a later signal, students switch to clapping the rhythm of the words, and so on. Students are alternately highlighting the beat or rhythm during the same performance of the newly-learned song.

• While singing a newly-learned song, invite students to walk in a line about the music room, to a steady beat, and clap the rhythm of the words simultaneously. If students experience difficulty with this, isolate one skill, for example, just stepping the beat, then at a later time, clap the rhythm of the words.

RHYTHMICALLY SPEAKING

• Notate the rhythm to a newly-learned song at the chalkboard or large chart. Invite students to clap it, and identify the song. Divide the singers into two groups: one group claps the rhythm forward in the usual manner; the other group claps the rhythm in reverse, simultaneously. With a big, all-knowing smile, pose this question before the students clap, and note the variety of student responses. Then, proceed with the activity:

"Which group will finish performing the rhythm first, the forward group, or the reverse group?"

• Invite students to focus on the written notation of a new song. Assign certain note values to be performed only by certain groups. For example:

   1) All quarter notes performed by the first row.
   2) All eighth notes performed by the second row.
   3) All half notes performed by the third row.
   4) All whole notes performed by the music teacher.

Or, invite half of the group to perform the first measure, the other half to perform the second measure, alternating measures throughout the song. A stereo effect is achieved! Switch roles and have musical fun!

• After a new song is introduced, notate all rhythms and/or melody on separate, flash card measures. Scramble. Allow the students to unscramble and sequence into proper order.

LET'S MOVE IT!

• With very young children whose songs are naturally accompanied by lots of motions, invite them to sing an entire song "inside their minds," while performing all motions on the "outside."

• Does the new song naturally invite accompanying motions? Allow students to brainstorm motions to fit certain words. Call out the action word, and observe the improvised motions. Choose one motion for the action word. Repeat with other selected words. This group of students truly owns the new song.

• Select a fairly short, known song. Design a different motion for each of several words throughout the song. Lead students through the singing of the song, and at the first selected word, substitute the motion for the sung word. In add-on fashion, continue to substitute more motions, one at a time, for selected, sung words. By the final rendition, the song sounds as if "it has holes in it." The holes are, of course, musical rests, visually represented by the substituted motions.

THE WHOLE IS THE SUM OF ITS PARTS

• Select a concept to emphasize in a newly-learned song. For example: *This Train Is Bound For Glory* contains the concept:

♪ ♩ ♪

(rhythmic speech: "syn-co-pah")

Instruct students to tap the beat with one foot, and inaudibly sing the entire song, except for the highlighted concept. This portion is sung aloud each time it occurs in the song. The only audible elements in the entire performance are the sound of the accompanying steady foot beat, and, the ever-so-often sung concept. With this tactic, students synthesize parts to the whole of the song.

TAKING TURNS

• During the rehearsal of a newly-learned song, establish a signal, such as a rap on the tone block. Divide singers into two groups. While all keep the steady beat of the song by clapping, tapping or patting, designate one group to start the singing. At the sound of the signal, the first group stops singing, while the other group resumes the singing of the song. Continue in this fashion, alternating groups at fairly predictable stopping points within the song, such as ends of phrases. Repeat, only sound the signal at unpredictable places in the song for fun and surprise.

> **"Beethoven possessed the ability to 'hear' all the music he composed, even though an illness caused him to become completely deaf. He heard music with his inside ears."**

• The "Think-Sing Flash cards":

1) Make two flash cards, one red, one green. On the green, mount a magazine picture of an animal with a wide-open mouth. Label in large letters: SING! On the red, mount a magazine picture of an animal with a tightly-shut mouth. Label in large letters: THINK!

2) Invite students to sing a newly-learned melody.

3) Ask students to repeat the melody and accompany it with a steady, tapping heartbeat. Whenever the SING! card is in view, sing audibly. Whenever the THINK! card is in view, switch to inaudible singing. Stress in-tune singing skills.

4) Gradually, increase the amount of time that the THINK! card is in view, until the only moments when the SING! card is exposed are the very first and last words of the song! Did students sing those two words in tune?

5) Ask students if they can still "hear" the song on the inside, even though it isn't sounding on the outside.

Describe to students the valuable technique of working the "inner ears" just like Beethoven did:

"Beethoven possessed the ability to 'hear' all the music he composed, even though an illness caused him to become completely deaf. He heard music with his inside ears."

• While clapping the same song rhythm, conduct half of the singers in rhythm clapping, and bring in the other half two beats, or one entire measure later. The effect is "round" or "canon-style" harmony.

OSTINATO OBBLIGATO

• Time to create. Encourage students to create a two or four measure rhythmic ostinato to accompany a newly-learned song. Notate the ostinato on a chalkboard or large chart. Divide singers into two groups. One group sings the song; the other group claps the ostinato. At your signal, both groups switch roles. Later, for more progressive challenge, conduct all singers through the clapping ostinato as an "introduction," and continue the ostinato throughout the performance of the song.

• Notate basic rhythm patterns on a series of flash cards in the same meter as a newly-learned song. Flash the cards during a performance of the newly-learned song. Students are challenged to sing the song, while at the same time clap the rhythms flashed before them, as an ostinato.

• For a harmonically-simple song, such as a round, or two-chord song, this technique quickly adds musical sophistication as well as challenge:

1) Select one phrase. For example, in the song *Are You Sleeping*, select the last phrase: *"ding dong ding."*
2) Create an ostinato by inviting half of the singing group to sing the phrase over and over.
3) At your signal, conduct the remaining singers through the song, while the first group continues the ostinato. An effective two-part harmony is achieved.
4) For fun and experimentation, augment or diminish the rhythm of the ostinato. Reinforce the sung ostinato by inviting selected students to play it on pitched instruments.

TRY TO REMEMBER

• At the chalkboard or large chart, print the words to learned, but not-yet-memorized songs. Invite students to sing the entire song. Erase one phrase of words. Sing again. Erase another measure of words. Sing again. Continue the process, until all words are "invisible" at the chalkboard, and "visible" only in the singers' minds!

• More memory fun:

1) While seated in a chair, students sit all around you, preferably down on the floor.
2) Invite them to close their eyes for the duration of the memory activity.
3) Lead students' through the first phrase of a newly-learned song.
4) Stop. Ask for a show of hands for any student who can sing the next phrase of words, aloud.
5) Select a student to sing the next phrase.
6) All echo.
7) Lead students in singing the cumulative first and second phrases.
8) Continue in this fashion until all phrases of words are committed to singers' memories.

9 MUSICAL LEARNING
OUTCOMES

ASSESSMENT METHODS

"**M**usic For All Children!" This caption appeared on a poster displayed in an elementary school music classroom. It is a noble goal, often voiced by elementary music educators as a kind of universal mission statement. In light of this concept, the following discussion examines the separate functions of assessment and evaluation and the way each measures student musical learning outcomes.

SHARED
RESPONSIBILITY

When musical learning outcomes are assessed and evaluated, who is the individual being assessed and evaluated? The obvious answer is of course, the music student. However, isn't the music educator also partly responsible for the music grade which he/she assigns? Can a correlation be made between the effectiveness of the music educator's teaching skills and the musical learning outcomes attained by the student? When a student is assessed and evaluated by the individual who provides the instruction, isn't assessment and evaluation really a shared process? For example:

"How well did I teach?" (Music Educator)
"How well did I learn?" (Music Student)

More questions arise. When a student's musical learning outcomes are assessed and evaluated, from whose perceptions, observations and calculations is the music grade usually formulated? It would appear of course, the music educator's. How is the music grade evaluation to be perceived and interpreted by the student? Does the music grade evaluation offer to the student useful information that:

1) assesses musical learning outcomes and/or musical growth?
2) nurtures the self-concept?
3) encourages future learning?

Let's consider the case of "Mark." Mark likes music and would like to learn to sing well, but a previous music teacher told him that he was tone deaf. What if Mark opens his mouth to sing, and for the very first time overcomes painful anxiety in doing so? If his current music teacher assigns a "D" grade to Mark, whose learning behavior (effort) shows a perceived lack of interest, and whose singing skills are monotone, how is this grade to be interpreted?

What does a grade of "D" do to Mark's learning attitude about music? Is it truly an appropriate grade which evaluates Mark's musical skills development? Development from whose reference point? Is it possible that Mark might perceive the development of his own musical skills from an entirely different angle than his teacher?

> **"Most music educators agree that music education, unlike other school subjects, is not a matter of cut-and-dried facts and formulas, but rather, a highly-interactive, sequential, developmental process, the unfolding and growth of which varies with each individual."**

ASSESS FIRST, EVALUATE LATER

These are two dictionary definitions:

Assess – to determine the rate or amount of...

Evaluate – to examine and judge; appraise...

In other words, to assess is to size up, and to evaluate is to rate or pass judgment. These two processes will be referred to throughout the duration of this chapter.

Most music educators agree that music education, unlike other school subjects, is not a matter of cut-and-dried facts and formulas, but rather, a highly-interactive, sequential, developmental process, the unfolding and growth of which varies with each individual. This individual growth process, involving a music student's higher-order, critical-thinking skills relative to listening, moving, reading, writing, playing, interpreting, sequencing, memorizing and creating music, is difficult (if not impossible) to measure with traditional systems of evaluation, typically used for other subject areas in elementary school. Traditional evaluation systems use percentages that conveniently and efficiently translate learning outcomes and effort into letter grades (A,B,C,D,F), or number grades (1,2,3,4,5), or word grades (Superior, Excellent, Very Good, Good, Fair, Poor, Fail).

It has been recognized that the quality of a student's self-concept is a significant factor in predicting his/her learning success in school. In light of this information, consider the following thought: To evaluate a student's musical learning outcomes (Excellent, Fair, Poor, etc.) is to DOUBLY impact on that individual's self-concept, which ultimately impacts on his/her learning success in school. Let's analyze. First, a student's self-concept is affected when that individual becomes aware of his/her ability or inability to perform a particular musical skill, for example, singing in tune. Next, the student's self-concept is again affected when the music educator evaluates the level of musical achievement attained by that individual. What do these thoughts imply for the music educator who undertakes the process of evaluating student musical achievement?

It is helpful for music educators whose classes typically meet once or twice per week, to think in terms of only assessing, not evaluating, student learning outcomes at the end of the quarter, term or semester grading periods. Then, evaluation might be judiciously undertaken only after much time has been spent for musical concepts to become internalized, and musical skills to become developed. And even then, a music grade evaluation should perhaps only measure an assessment of the student's current musical learning outcomes against a prior assessment of the student's past musical learning outcomes. See section titled *Self-Referenced Norms Vs. Group-Referenced Norms* on page 155.

> **"'Music For All Children' can sadly become music for only select children."**

Let's examine the skill of playing a rhythmic ostinato on a hand drum, or the skill of singing in harmony with others. These skills are acquired by children who possess varied musical aptitudes, over varying amounts of time, with varying degrees of success. Some acquire these skills with astonishing, immediate success. Others develop these skills only after repeated practice over long spans of time. Still others develop only minimal musical skills, all the while enjoying self-expression, and appreciating the therapeutic benefits derived from the process of making music. When music educators evaluate musical learning outcomes in the spirit of "remediating students' musical weaknesses," they can inadvertently undernourish children's musical potentials, or discourage them from developing at all. "Music For All Children" can sadly become music for only select children.

A musical phenomenon exists among certain children who have autism. Children who happen to be autistic have been known to acquire perfect pitch, memorize incredible amounts of music, or play a piece of piano music with complete accuracy upon hearing it for the first time. It is obvious that significant alterations in mental function and emotional health are unrelated to musical aptitude. What does this wide variance in children's musical aptitudes suggest to the music educator undertaking the process of evaluating student musical achievement?

> "It is obvious that significant alterations in mental function and emotional health are unrelated to musical aptitude."

Let's take the case of "Robby." Robby possesses a motor disability which impacts on his ability to express himself through music as freely as some of his peers. Robby loves music class, although his movement participation is somewhat limited. Robby's self-concept could be shattered if he received a "Poor" evaluation regarding his musical skills development. Could Robby's musical skills development be only assessed, and not evaluated, thus eliminating the need to judge or rate his musical learning outcomes? By observing the frequency with which he attempts to appropriately perform certain musical skills, Robby's development and performance can be personally and individually assessed. After much time, future assessments of Robby's musical skill development could be measured against his past assessments in order to appropriately evaluate his own, individual, musical learning growth.

For elementary music educators who are in the business of nurturing the musical potentials in all children ("Music For All Children"), early evaluation of children's musical achievements might well be a risky undertaking. The process is considered risky if it could invariably damage a child's learning attitude about him/herself and the process of making music. If student musical learning outcomes are assessed first, and musical growth is evaluated later by measuring a student's current learning outcomes against prior learning outcomes, then the evaluation process is educationally safe and sound. In this manner, a child's musical learning outcomes are assessed, a child's self-concept is nurtured, and a child's future learning success is ultimately encouraged.

SELF-REFERENCED NORMS
VS. GROUP-REFERENCED NORMS

Imagine that a student acquires musical knowledge and skills according to his/her own "personal, musical developmental continuum." In order to truly evaluate an individual's improvement and growth in musical learning outcomes, a method which assesses his/her placement along that continuum, and measures it against an earlier placement, is necessary. Evaluation in this manner is accomplished over time, by measuring a student's current acquisition of musical knowledge and skills against his/her own "self-referenced norm."

In contrast, a group-grading scale, or "curve" is typically determined by many elementary school educators, based on the high, median and low learning outcomes of a particular student group. This "group-referenced norm" becomes the "measuring stick" against which a student's academic achievement is typically measured and evaluated. Grading a music student from this perspective, unfortunately disregards the individual's "personal, musical development continuum." Music evaluation against a group-referenced norm ultimately measures the musical learning outcomes of each student against one, collective musical barometer. It appears to contradict the very approach so many music educators choose through which they educate their students to uniquely experience, express and appreciate music as a creative art form.

> *"Imagine that a student acquires musical knowledge and skills according to his/her own 'personal, musical developmental continuum.'"*

PRODUCTS OF EFFECTIVE MUSIC TEACHING

In music class, what are the observable and measurable products (or musical learning outcomes) of effective music teaching? Certainly, there are two – a student's development and acquisition of:

1) Musical skills (as assessed through observation of performed musical skills).
2) Musical knowledge (as assessed with a verbal and/or written recall of learned musical concepts).

A by-product of effective music teaching is a music student's development and acquisition of :

3) Appropriate learning behaviors in the music room (as assessed through observation of learning behaviors).

ASSESSMENT METHODS

Following are three methods which can be used to assess students' musical learning outcomes:

A) THE OBSERVABLE MUSIC SKILLS ASSESSMENT METHOD

The Observable Music Skills Assessment Method assesses a student's musical learning outcomes regarding his/her development and performance of musical skills. Imagine a group of upper-elementary students developing and performing, for example, these musical skills:

• Performs rhythms in 6/8 with relative accuracy
• Sings in tune with others in a two-part canon
• Moves in rhythm to choreography
• Sings with stylistic dynamic and tempo expression in vocal performance
• Discerns harmonic changes from I chord to V7 chord

Unlike the highly objective evaluation process used for other academic subjects, which involves the compiling, tallying, scoring and recording of concrete test scores, the evaluation of a music student's development and performance of musical skills is a highly subjective process. It is most appropriate to assess this individual's musical skills development through direct observation of his/her performance, and noting WHAT the student performs, and the FREQUENCY with which he/she attempts to appropriately perform it. With the Observable Skills Assessment Method, the music teacher assesses the frequency with which a student attempts to appropriately perform certain musical skills during a particular quarter, term or semester grading period, without evaluating a perceived level of success.

Please note the form titled, *Assessment of Musical Learning Outcomes* on page 161. This report form can accompany the student's regular report card. Musical concepts and skills which were presented during that particular grading period can be listed on the form. The assessment of musical skills development and performance is presented on the top portion of the form in this manner:

"During lessons which stressed the development and performance of musical skills (singing, playing, moving, creating), this student was observed appropriately performing the following skills:"

The Assessment Key describes the frequency at which a student is observed appropriately performing certain musical skills:

Consistently
Frequently
Occasionally
Rarely
Not Yet

The area designated for Comments can include information which describes the student's learning behaviors and/or recommendations for increased challenge and/or improvement.

B) THE EARNED POINTS ASSESSMENT METHOD

The Earned Points Assessment Method assesses a student's musical learning outcomes regarding his/her acquisition of musical knowledge. Now, imagine that same group of upper-elementary students involved in a semester unit of music theory. By its very nature, this type of musical learning outcome is more objectively assessed. At the start of the unit, the music teacher presents students with an outline of points which can be earned or lost with:

1) Course assignments ("practice pages").
2) Tests.
3) Extra credit bonus opportunities.
4) Late, incomplete or incorrect items (penalty points).

For example:

1) Five "practice page" assignments: (5 points each)	= 25 points
2) One written test:	= 15 points
TOTAL POINTS:	40 points
3) Two extra credit opportunities: (5 points each)	= 10 points
TOTAL POSSIBLE POINTS WITH EXTRA CREDIT:	50 points
4) One penalty point subtracted per each:	
a) incomplete or incorrect item on "practice page" and/or written test.	
b) late day "practice page."	

With the Earned Points Assessment Method, a student accumulates points during a particular quarter, term or semester grading period. Please note the form titled, *Assessment of Musical Learning Outcomes* on page 161. This report form can accompany the student's regular report card. Musical concepts which were presented during that particular grading period can be listed on the form. Assessing acquisition of musical knowledge is done by tallying the total number of accumulated points, and recording that number on the lower portion of the form in this manner:

"During lessons which stressed the acquisition of musical knowledge (theory, history, appreciation), this student accumulated _____ points out of _____ possible points.

The area designated for Comments can include information which describes a student's learning behaviors and/or recommendations for increased challenge and/or improvement.

Please refer to the section titled, *My Very Own Music Book* on page 37. Throughout the school year, each student's "practice pages," songs, theory sheets, tests, extra credit assignments and more, are compiled and stored in his/her own music folder. This folder provides the music teacher with an efficient and convenient means for tallying earned points, and assessing individual student learning outcomes.

C) THE SELF-ASSESSMENT METHOD

With the Self-Assessment Method, the musical skills developed during a particular quarter, term or semester grading period, can be listed on the page titled, *Shared Assessment of Musical Learning Outcomes* on page 162. At the onset of the grading period, the music teacher discusses this assessment strategy with students. Throughout the grading period, each student has the opportunity to pay attention to his/her own development and performance of musical skills, and take personal responsibility for assessing his/her musical skills development. This report form can accompany the student's regular report card. Invite each student to self-assess his/her own musical skills development on the report form. Then, next to each student's assessment, add your assessment. Compare. In cases where a significant discrepancy in assessments in evident, invite the student to conference with you. Insight into a student's learning attitude and learning capabilities is gained for the sensitive music educator who chooses this approach.

NON-ASSESSMENT, NON-EVALUATION

For some music educators, assessment and/or evaluation of student musical learning outcomes can be an unrealistic, impractical and frustrating activity. Conscientious assessment and evaluation of the growth of musical learning outcomes is virtually impossible for the music educator who:

1) must provide music instruction to an overwhelming number of students, for example, 1000 students weekly, or
2) provides music instruction to a large number of students only once a week or bi-weekly.

It is enough challenge to personalize music instruction to large numbers of students while trying to remember their names, and rather than succumb to guesswork, it is beneficial for the music educator to eliminate assessment and evaluation, altogether. The following option can be considered. Along with the student's regular report card, a reproduced report may be sent which lists the musical concepts and skills stressed during a particular quarter, term or semester grading period. Please note the form titled *Musical Learning Outcomes* on page 160. This report form describes the content of musical instruction provided by the music educator during the grading period, as well as the musical learning outcomes. The reader is informed of the many, diverse musical activities to which the child has been exposed.

Name: _____ Date:_____

Grade Level:_____ Class: _____

Dear Parent:

In music class, your child takes part in an active, musical learning experience which includes singing, playing, memorizing, reading, writing, creating, listening to, and appreciating music. Through these activities, your child acquires musical knowledge and skills that can help him/her enjoy and make music now and in the future.

Thank you for your support of our music program.

Sincerely,

_____

Music Teacher

CONCEPT

**MUSICAL LEARNING OUTCOMES
(KNOWLEDGE AND SKILLS)**

(This page may be photocopied.)

MUSICAL LEARNING OUTCOMES

Name: _____   Date: _____
Grade Level: _____   Class: _____

Dear Parent:

In music class, your child takes part in an active, musical learning experience which includes singing, playing, memorizing, reading, writing, creating, listening to, and appreciating music. Through these activities, your child acquires musical knowledge and skills that can help him/her enjoy and make music now and in the future.

Thank you for your support of our music program.

Sincerely,

_____

Music Teacher

MUSICAL SKILLS ASSESSMENT

During lessons which stressed the development and performance of musical skills (singing, playing, moving, etc.), this student was observed performing the following skills in an appropriate manner:

CONCEPT	SKILLS (MUSICAL LEARNING OUTCOMES)	ASSESSMENT
_____	_____	_____
_____	_____	_____
_____	_____	_____
_____	_____	_____
_____	_____	_____
_____	_____	_____

ASSESSMENT KEY: Consistently, Frequently, Occasionally, Rarely, Not Yet

MUSICAL KNOWLEDGE ASSESSMENT

During lessons which stressed the acquisition of musical knowledge (theory, history, appreciation, etc.), this student accumulated _____ points out of _____ possible points.

CONCEPT	KNOWLEDGE (MUSICAL LEARNING OUTCOMES)
_____	_____
_____	_____
_____	_____
_____	_____
_____	_____
_____	_____

Comments: _____
_____

ASSESSMENT OF MUSICAL LEARNING OUTCOMES

Name: _____   Date: _____

Grade Level: _____   Class: _____

Dear Parent:

In music class, your child takes part in an active, musical learning experience which includes singing, playing, memorizing, reading, writing, creating, listening to, and appreciating music. Through these activities, your child acquires musical knowledge and skills that can help him/her enjoy and make music now and in the future.

Thank you for your support of our music program.

Sincerely,

_____

Music Teacher

MUSICAL SKILLS ASSESSMENT

During lessons which stressed the development and performance of musical skills (singing, playing, moving, etc.), this student was observed performing the following skills in an appropriate manner:

CONCEPT	SKILLS (MUSICAL LEARNING OUTCOMES)	SELF-ASSESSMENT	TEACHER-ASSESSMENT
_____	_____	_____	_____
_____	_____	_____	_____
_____	_____	_____	_____
_____	_____	_____	_____
_____	_____	_____	_____
_____	_____	_____	_____

ASSESSMENT KEY: Consistently, Frequently, Occasionally, Rarely, Not Yet

MUSICAL KNOWLEDGE ASSESSMENT

During lessons which stressed the acquisition of musical knowledge (theory, history, appreciation, etc.), this student accumulated _____ points out of _____ possible points.

CONCEPT	KNOWLEDGE (MUSICAL LEARNING OUTCOMES)
_____	_____
_____	_____
_____	_____
_____	_____
_____	_____
_____	_____

Comments: _____

_____

SHARED ASSESSMENT OF MUSICAL LEARNING OUTCOMES

(This page may be photocopied.)

NEGATIVE LEARNING OUTCOMES

WHEN EFFECTIVE MUSIC TEACHING DOESN'T HAPPEN

When a music student shows evidence of negative learning outcomes, the sensitive music educator is compelled to search for the causes. A negative assessment of a student's musical learning outcomes may not reflect the efforts of the student alone. Sometimes, a negative assessment is shared by the music educator, as well. Referring to the section titled *Effective Music Teaching* on page 2, the sensitive music educator first looks within, and measures his/her teaching performance against the criteria which must be met in order to qualify as effective music teaching:

▶ *"A negative assessment of a student's musical learning outcomes may not reflect the efforts of the student alone."*

1) A child's self-esteem is addressed.
2) A child is made aware of course content and learning expectations (learning outcomes are the result of the actual teaching/learning experience).
3) A child's learning readiness level and individual learning style are accurately assessed, and included in researching, planning, preparing and delivering the music lesson.
4) The top priority for a child in each music lesson is not WHAT to learn but HOW to learn.
5) A child's curiosity is aroused, and attention is captivated through the use of varied, motivational techniques.
6) A child's use of critical-thinking skills and decision-making skills is continually encouraged.
7) A child's musical efforts are continually encouraged.
8) A child's improvement and growth in the acquisition of musical knowledge and skills, and other learning behaviors, is periodically assessed.

If changes or adaptations in the music educator's teaching skills need to be made in order to help remediate negative learning outcomes, the sensitive music educator initiates his/her own research and change. Music educators in search of additional teaching methods and techniques can acquire fresh, new strategies and perspectives by joining professional organizations, attending workshops and inservices, observing master music educators, and networking with local music educators.

> "Music educators can acquire fresh, new strategies and perspectives by joining professional organizations, attending workshops and inservices, observing master music educators, and networking with local music educators."

WHEN EFFECTIVE MUSICAL LEARNING DOESN'T HAPPEN

When the criteria for effective music teaching is met, and a student's musical learning outcomes continue to be negatively assessed, the focus of concern shifts from the teacher to the student. Questions arise:

• Does the student regularly attend music class, but refuses to participate in any way?

• Does the student repeatedly display behaviors which purposely interfere with his/her own improvement and growth in learning, even though it may not interfere with others' learning?

• Does the student perceive a personality clash with the music teacher which prevents them from bonding in a nurturing teacher/student relationship?

• Has the student undergone a major life-style change?

• Has the student been involved in a neglectful or abusive home setting?

• Has the student earned more than two or three C.Y.B. assignments because of repeated, learning-disruptive behavior? (See section titled, "Dealing With Inappropriate Behavior - The C.Y.B." on page 22.)

• Has the student's behavior required monitoring and supervision with use of the MUSI-CONTRACT? (See page 25.)

• Does the student appear to lack feeling, regard or conscience concerning a learning-disruptive situation which he/she has initiated?

• Does the student appear to be angry much of the time, and exhibit unpredictable mood changes?

• Does the student appear to have few or no friends?

If answers to these questions are "yes" or "maybe," then the student fitting this description possibly possesses severe emotional/behavioral concerns, the diagnosis and treatment of which are beyond the realm of educational expertise possessed by the very best of elementary music educators.

Assessment of musical learning outcomes may be next to impossible with this type of student, and it may be necessary to employ an alternative strategy. If the student has been in attendance at regular music classes, yet has been unwilling to participate in any manner, he/she receives an assessment of: AUD (Audience). It is an alternative assessment which implies that the student earned zero credit, and assesses his/her participation in music class as a learning audience, rather than a learning participant.

WHOLE-GROUP MUSIC ASSESSMENT GAMES

MUSI-QUEST

MUSI-QUEST is a make-it-yourself, quick-paced, whole-group music game which is played to assess students' acquisition of both musical knowledge and skills. MUSI-QUEST is played by an entire group of music students at the same time. It may be played at any grade level, by simply changing the Quest Cards in the numbered packets. All students respond to an equal number of Quest Cards. The number of Quest Cards is determined by the teacher. Quest Cards require either a verbal or performance response. (The MUSI-QUEST materials can be made with the assistance of parent or student helpers, as considerable time and effort are required for construction.) Once the game is assembled, it can be played time and time again.

- Materials:

    - one MUSI-QUEST game board (construction tips on page 168)
    - one set of Quest Cards (instructions for making on page 169)
    - four Bonus Cards (instructions for making on page 170)
    - two Penalty Cards (instructions for making on page 170)
    - two pair dice (cover the "one dot" on one die in each pair with white enamel
    - one highly-visible, Whole-Group Score Chart and marker (can be chalkboard or large, wipe-away chart)
    - one set of individual, student Score-Keepers for Points Attempted (?)
    - one set of individual, student Score-Keepers for Points Earned (*)
    - musical equipment, such as rhythm instruments, staff liner and chalk, song bells, piano, etc. as per the questions on the Quest Cards
    - stickers or certificates of participation, as desired (certificate on page 205)

•Object of the Game:

The music teacher designates a number of "goal" points to be earned cumulatively by the whole group. Students earn points with correct responses to the Quest Cards contained in the numbered packets. If the goal is reached, a group prize is offered. (Group prizes can include: stickers, stamps, the playing of favorite records or videos, musical "choice" day, and others, as deemed appropriate by the music teacher.) If students are unable to reach the goal, stickers or certificates of participation are awarded for effort. The number of individual score-keepers indicating points earned (*), received by each student is recorded - this tally assesses his/her musical learning outcomes.

• Directions for Play:

1) Determine order of players.
2) First player rolls dice and calls out the number of exposed dots.
3) The teacher draws a Quest Card from the corresponding numbered packet on the MUSI-QUEST game board. For example, a dice roll of four indicates a draw from the number four packet on the game board.
4) The teacher draws the Quest Card from the packet and reads the printed question or command. The student responds. If correct, the teacher prints the number of dice roll on the score chart, and the student takes an individual score-keeper, indicating points earned (*). The teacher returns the Quest Card to the numbered packet, at the rear of the stack. It sometimes happens that, throughout the duration of the game, the entire stack of Quest Cards from one packet is used, and the same Quest Cards are shown for a second time.
5) If the student responds incorrectly, he/she takes an individual score-keeper, indicating points attempted (?). The same Quest Card automatically goes to the next player in turn.
6) The next student in turn does not roll the dice, but responds to the same Quest Card. If correct, the teacher prints the number of dice roll on the score chart, and this student takes an individual score-keeper, indicating points earned (*).
7) The same Quest Card may be passed to a maximum of three students. If a correct response is not yet given, the Quest Card may be offered to any player. If a correct response is given, the whole-group score is moved ahead the number of the dice roll. If no one is able to respond correctly, the teacher provides the correct response, and the Quest Card is returned to the rear of the numbered packet.

8) Whenever a correct response is given to a Quest Card, the next student in turn always begins his/her turn by rolling the dice.

9) The game continues in this fashion, with the teacher adding the number of the dice roll for each correct response to the group score, until every student has answered an equal number of questions. Lesson time naturally limits the number of Quest Cards. A half-hour lesson with 25 players may yield five Quest Cards per student, and continuing the game the following music lesson could yield a total of ten Quest Cards per student.

10) At the conclusion of the game, the number of each student's individual score-keepers, indicating points earned (*) is tallied. The teacher privately records each student's tally as an individual assessment of his/her musical learning outcomes. The whole-group score is tallied, and determination for group prize, stickers or certificates is made.

• Bonus Cards:

1) When a card which shows (:‖) is drawn, the student responds to the Quest Card behind it in the stack, then REPEATS, and responds to the next Quest Card behind it (a total of two Quest Cards). If the student responds correctly both times, the teacher moves the score ahead by TWICE the dice roll. A double-score bonus!

2) If the response to the second Quest Card is incorrect, the score moves ahead only the exact amount of the actual dice roll, and the student takes an individual score keeper, indicating points earned (*). If the student responds correctly to both Quest Cards, he/she only takes only one individual score-keeper, indicating points earned (*).

3) If the student responds incorrectly to the first Quest Card, it automatically goes to the next player in order, and this student "inherits" the same opportunity for earning a double score. The Quest Card may be passed to a maximum of three players before it is offered to any player. (At this point, the double-score bonus is cancelled.) If the correct response is given, the number of the original dice roll is added to the whole-group score. If an incorrect response is given, the teacher provides the correct response, and the Quest Card is returned to the rear of the numbered packet.

• Penalty Cards:

1) When a card which shows (⌢) is drawn, the student answers the Quest Card behind it in the stack. If correct, the student takes an individual score-keeper, indicating points earned (*), but the whole-group score HOLDS, and does not advance. If the response is incorrect, the student takes an individual score-keeper, indicated points attempted (?), and the next player in order "inherits" the same turn.

2) The Quest Card may be passed to a maximum of three players, before it is offered to any player. If an incorrect response is given, the teacher provides the correct response, and the Quest Card is returned to the rear of the numbered packet.

• Game Board Construction Tips:

1) Obtain a cardboard easel (This can be purchased from most office supply stores.)

2) Obtain 12 small envelopes. (If desired, colorful envelopes are especially attractive.) Cut off the flap of each envelope. Using black marker, number each envelope, one through twelve. These are the numbered packets.

3) Design the placement of each numbered packet on the face of the game board as shown, or use your own creative game board design.

4) Attach numbered packets to the game board, reinforcing upper edges. Into each packet goes an equal number of Quest Cards.

5) Label game board MUSI-QUEST.

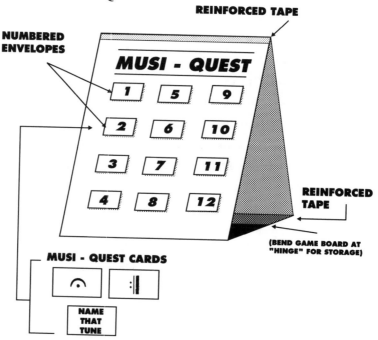

• Instructions For Making Quest Cards:

1) Determine the number of Quest Cards needed for the game. For example, with a group of 25 students, each responding to 10 Quest Cards, the number of Quest Cards to make should be 250. (There are 12 numbered packets, so that calculates out to over 20 cards per packet.) However, making this many cards would require an impractical amount of preparation time. It is not necessary for the game to contain the same number of Quest Cards as there are student responses, because Quest Cards can be drawn more than once. It is recommended that Quest Cards be repeated, especially performance ones, so that students hear musical questions and correct answers more than once, for additional learning reinforcement. So, each numbered packet could contain say, seven to ten Quest Cards, yielding 84 to 120 cards in all.

2) Cut out the number of Quest Cards needed for the game from regular paper. The size of the Quest Cards must fit inside the numbered packets on the game board.

3) Choose topics for Quest Cards which cover the unit of music study being assessed. MUSI-QUEST works especially well for assessing end of quarter, term or semester musical learning outcomes.

4) On each Quest Card, print or notate a brief musical question or statement. For example:

Clap:

Name the musical term which means "very loud": *(ff - fortissimo)*

Name That Tune: (Teacher sings or plays part of a known melody.)

Define: composer

Interpret the meter signature 2/4:

Sing the first two phrases of the National Anthem

Play on bells:

5) It is helpful to color-code the deck of Quest Cards for each level of play. For example, sixth grade students play with blue Quest Cards, while third graders play with yellow cards. It is an efficient way to keep the decks of Quest Cards separate.

6) Determine the number of Quest Cards to be placed in each numbered packet on the game board. For example, a total of 120 cards calculates out to 10 cards per packet. Place Quest Cards in packets.

• Instructions For Making Bonus/Penalty Cards:

Four Bonus Cards is usually about right for a 30 minute game, however, more or less can be used. Cut out cards the same size as the Quest Cards, and on each one, draw the symbol: :‖

Cut out two Penalty Cards, and on each one, draw the symbol: ⌒

Place the Bonus Cards and Penalty Cards in the numbered packets randomly throughout the game board.

• Instructions For Whole-Group Score Chart:

Use a large poster, wipe-away chart, or chalkboard for scoring correct student responses. With each correct response, add to the existing score the actual number of dots from the dice roll. At the conclusion of the game, the score shows the total number of points earned by the group's cumulative, correct responses to the Quest Cards.

• Instructions For Making Individual Score-Keepers:

Using card stock and a paper cutter, quickly slice individual markers approximately this size: 1" x 5." The number of markers is determined by the maximum number of anticipated student responses. For example, if 25 students each answer 10 questions, then make sure to have 500 markers available, 250 on which are printed: (?), indicating points attempted, and 250 on which are printed: (*), indicating points earned. For greater durability, markers may be laminated.

MUSIC ROUND ROBIN

MUSIC ROUND ROBIN is a make-it-yourself, quick-paced, whole-group game which is played to reinforce and assess whole-group acquisition of musical knowledge. MUSIC ROUND ROBIN is a timed activity which challenges each student to answer musical questions as fast as they can. A set of calling cards is made up by the music teacher ahead of time, with minimal preparation. MUSIC ROUND ROBIN is played by an entire group of music students at the same time.

• Materials:

   • one set of numbered, sequenced calling cards (standard 4" x 6" index cards. Instructions for printed information on cards on page 173.)
   • one stopwatch

• Object of the Game:

Students attempt to progress through MUSIC ROUND ROBIN within a designated time limit. Teacher determines time limit, say five minutes, gradually shortening the time limit with each, subsequent play of the game. If the round robin is completed within the time limit, a group prize is offered. (Prizes can be stickers, stamps, certificates of participation, the playing of favorite records, tapes or videos, a musical "choice" day, or other prizes deemed appropriate by the music teacher.)

• Directions for Play:

   1) Sequence the numbered calling cards. Determine the number of players, and use the same number of calling cards. For example, if the set consists of 25 calling cards, and there are only 23 players, simply remove the last two cards from the deck.
   2) The calling cards are shuffled and distributed, one to each player.
   3) The starting player is the student holding the first calling card.
   4) Teacher calls: "Ready, set, go!," and begins timing the round robin with a stop watch.
   5) The starting player reads aloud the statement on the front side of the first calling card, then flips the card over and reads aloud the question on the reverse side. For example, "I am a quarter note. (front side) What note gets two times my value?" (reverse side)

6) All players quickly search the fronts of their calling cards for the correct answer to the question.

7) The player whose card shows the correct answer, immediately reads it aloud. For example, "I am a half-note." He/she then flips the card over and immediately reads the question on the reverse side.

8) The game continues in this fashion. The game is concluded after the last player reads aloud the question on his/her calling card, and the starting player reads the corresponding answer on the first calling card (remember, this was the first statement made at the beginning of the round robin). The round robin has run its course, and each player has responded. (In the event that some cards are removed from the deck, due to fewer players than the number of calling cards, the teacher answers the last player's question, as the card which shows the corresponding answer has been removed.)

9) Immediately upon hearing the last answer, the teacher calls: "Time!" and stops the stopwatch. The teacher announces the number of minutes taken for the duration of MUSIC ROUND ROBIN, and determines eligibility for the group prize.

• Instructions For Making Calling Cards:

1) Determine the number of students in your largest playing group, and obtain the same number of 4" x 6" index cards. (For example, if you teach four class sections of fifth grade, and the largest group numbers 26, obtain 26 index cards. When playing MUSIC ROUND ROBIN with the remaining fifth grade groups, remove as many cards as necessary from the end of the deck, so that there are exactly the same number of cards as players.)

2) Number each card in sequence. On the reverse side of the first card, print a question. On the front of the second card, print the answer which corresponds to the question on the first card. Continue, until the printed answer on the first card corresponds to the printed question on the last card.

Following is a sample set of calling cards for a basic music theory game. It is age-appropriate for upper-elementary music students. Use your own imagination to create many MUSIC ROUND ROBINS based on music history, musical styles, elements of music, composers, famous songs or musical works, and more.

1) Front: I am an eighth note (♪).
   Reverse: What music note gets twice my value?

2) Front: I am a quarter note (♩).
   Reverse: What music note gets three times my value?

3) Front: I am a dotted half note (♩.).
   Reverse: What music note gets the same value as me, plus one more beat?

4) Front: I am a whole note (o).
   Reverse: What music note gets half my value?

5) Front: I am half note (♩.).
   Reverse: If two of me are tied together, how many beats do I get?

6) Front: I am the number 4.
   Reverse: If two of me are stacked on top of one another at the beginning of notated music, what am I called?

7) Front: I am a time signature (4/4).
   Reverse: What does my bottom number tell?

8) Front: I am a music note that equals one beat of music.
   Reverse: What does the top number of the time signature tell?

9) Front: I am the number of beats in each measure of music.
   Reverse: What is a measure?

10) Front: I am a unit of musical notation.
    Reverse: What kind of line separates me from other measures?

11) Front: I am a bar line. (|)
    Reverse: There are two of me at the end of a section of notated music. What am I called?

12) Front: I am a double bar line. (‖)

Reverse: What is the term for the "stick" part of a music note?

13) Front: I am a stem. (|)

Reverse: I am the round part connected to the stem of a music note. What am I?

14) Front: I am a note head. (•)

Reverse: What is the term for the "bridge" part which connects two eighth notes?

15) Front: I am a beam. (⌐)

Reverse: Name the Italian term for the first pitch of the major scale.

16) Front: I am *do*.

Reverse: Name the pitch that sounds two pitches higher than me.

17) Front: I am *mi*.

Reverse: Name the pitch that sounds two pitches higher than me.

18) Front: I am *so*.

Reverse: Name the pitch that sounds one pitch higher than me.

19) Front: I am *la*.

Reverse: Name the pitch that sounds two pitches lower than me.

20) Front: I am *fa*.

Reverse: Name the pitch that sounds two pitches lower than me.

21. Front: I am *re*.

Reverse: Name the seventh pitch of the major scale.

22. Front: I am *ti*.

Reverse: What is the distance between the first pitch and the eighth pitch of the major scale called?

23. Front: I am an octave.

Reverse: What is the name given to the five lines and four spaces upon which music notes live?

24. Front: I am a music staff. (≣≣)

   Reverse: Name the music symbol that lives on me and shows where "G" lives?

25. Front: I am a treble clef. (𝄞≣)

   Reverse: Name the music symbol that lives on me and shows where "F" lives.

26) Front: I am a bass clef (𝄢≣).

   Reverse: What kind of music note gets the value of one-half beat? (Remember, the answer to this question is on the front of the very first card.)

MUSIC-TAC-TOE

MUSIC-TAC-TOE is a make-it-yourself, quick-paced, whole-group game which is played to assess students' acquisition of both musical knowledge and skills. MUSIC-TAC-TOE is played by an entire group of music students at the same time. It may be played at any grade level, by simply changing the questions.

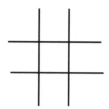 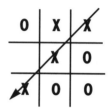

• Materials:

- chalkboard, or large, wipe-away chart on which is drawn a tic-tac-toe diagram (please note illustration)
- chalk or marker
- list of questions or commands compiled by the music teacher (instructions for making list of questions on page 173)
- musical equipment, such as: rhythm instruments, staff liner and chalk, song bells, piano, etc. as per the list of questions
- score chart (chalkboard or large chart)

• Object of the Game:

Two cooperative groups of students attempt to build a musical "tic-tac-toe" with correct answers to musical questions. In advance, the music teacher designates the cumulative number of "tic-tac-toes" which must be built during a designated time period in order for everyone to earn a whole-group prize. (Prizes can be stickers, stamps, certificates of participation, the playing of favorite records, tapes or videos, a musical "choice" day, or other prize ideas deemed appropriate by the music teacher.)

• Directions For Play:

1) Divide the student group into two cooperative groups: the X's and the O's.
2) Determine starting group (X's) and order of players.
3) Starting player from group X takes chalk (or marker). The teacher presents the first question to the starting player. If the student answers correctly, he/she draws an X in any selected space on the MUSIC-TAC-TOE diagram.

4) The starting player hands the chalk to the starting player from group O. The second question is presented to this player, and the game continues in this fashion.

5) If the starting player from group X answers the question incorrectly, the same question is repeated to the starting player from group O. If answered correctly, this player marks an O in any selected space on the MUSIC-TAC-TOE diagram. If answered incorrectly, the same question is repeated to the next player in turn from group X.

6) The same question can be presented to a maximum of three players. If answered incorrectly, the question may be offered to any player. If answered correctly, no mark is made on the MUSIC-TAC-TOE diagram. If answered incorrectly, the teacher offers the correct answer, and repeats the question at a later time in the game.

7) This round of MUSIC-TAC-TOE is concluded when one of the groups builds a "tic-tac-toe" on the MUSIC-TAC-TOE diagram. A "tic-tac-toe" shows three marks from one group forming a row either horizontally, vertically or diagonally. Please note illustration on p. 176.

8) When a "tic-tac-toe" is built on the MUSIC-TAC-TOE diagram, the teacher scores one point on the score board, and a subsequent round begins. A fresh MUSIC-TAC-TOE diagram is drawn, and the players in turn, resume the game, from the place where the previous round stopped.

9) MUSIC-TAC-TOE is concluded when the designated time period is over. The teacher tallies the total number of "tic-tac-toes," and determines eligibility for the group prize.

10 MAKING THE MUSIC ROOM OUR OWN

PERSONALIZING THE MUSICAL EXPERIENCE

Consider this thought shared during a parenting class: a child cannot be expected to share something with other individuals if he/she has not yet experienced ownership of the object for sharing. In other words, it is difficult for a child to learn the concept of sharing, if the concept of ownership is not already learned. How can one share something one does not own? This hypothesis is put to test when a child is expected to share his/her toys, food, games, turns, thoughts, feelings, friends, grown-ups and more. The perception: "Something that I own belongs to me, and I make the conscious choice about how it will be used and shared," is basic to all human beings, and crucial to children who are in the process of learning it.

> "Shared ownership of the musical experience breeds in children an attitude of sharing, and willingness to accept responsibility for the care and nurturing of this unique 'possession.'"

Who owns the music room? Does the music lesson belong to the teacher, or to the students? The direction of this focus largely shapes children's personal perceptions of music class. The purpose of this chapter is to suggest that children who truly feel shared ownership of the experience of music class more readily embrace the notion of sharing books, instruments, ideas, songs, solos, jobs, equipment, turns, or even, upholding the principles of the music room. When children perceive shared ownership of, and shared managerial control over the experiences in the music room, they need not be coerced by the music teacher into compliant, appropriate social conduct. Shared ownership of the musical experience breeds in children an attitude of sharing, and willingness to accept responsibility for the care and nurturing of this unique "possession."

Following are descriptions of music room activities and management roles which can be delegated to students by music teachers. The sensitive music teacher delegates only as much responsibility as his/her students are capable of handling, with gradual earned increases. The music teacher plays the somewhat invisible role of "stabilizer": a calm yet powerful, connecting force, like the tiny thread that holds together a patchwork quilt of hundreds of colorful pieces. With a patchwork quilt, one doesn't notice the thread. Instead, one focuses on the design and play of original, artful pieces.

> **"The music teacher plays the somewhat invisible role of 'stabilizer,' a calm yet powerful, connecting force, like the tiny thread that holds together a patchwork quilt."**

Add to this list of ideas your own unique activities which can personalize the music room for your students while putting them at the center of their own musical learning experiences.

MUSIC ROOM MANAGERS

Here is a starter list of music room jobs which can be executed by a rotating number of students. If desired, a wipe-away chart can show the names of students who currently hold these positions. A student who is unable to handle a role with appropriate responsibility is given the option of a second chance, or selecting another classmate to carry out the role. Students who achieve success in their respective roles earn a "badge" or certificate of achievement.

• Host/Hostess: This person greets anyone who should happen to appear at the music room door during a music lesson, so that the music teacher can continue teaching. This student offers: "Hi. My name is (student). Welcome to the music room. Mr. (teacher) is teaching right now. May I help you with something, or if necessary, may I get him for you?"

• Warm-Up Manager: In the event the music teacher is detained with other teaching-related business, this person conducts the music group through a series of routine singing/breathing/moving warm-up exercises at the beginning of music class. (See Ch. 7, p. 121.)

• Teaching Assistants: These persons tutor fellow students who require learning assistance. With increased mainstreaming of special education children and increased cross-cultural and ethnic diversity in the classroom, "students helping students" is a concept which enables students to help one another, while allowing the teacher to carry out instructional activities beneficial to the entire group. Older students are invited to attend early childhood music classes, to assist little bodies.

• Technical Assistant: This person operates the turntable, tape player and C.D. player during music lessons.

• Conductor: This person leads the singing of the opening and closing song of the music lesson, and could conduct one song for a performance or program.

• Service Technicians: These persons assist in the cleaning/repairing of classroom instruments, supplies, books, music, equipment, and more. They also assist the music teacher with cutting, pasting, checking papers, clearing chalkboards, etc.

• Concept-Chart Assistant: This person draws the concept of the music lesson on the chalkboard or large wipe-away chart. The concept might be a musical symbol, accompanied by its Italian term (⌢ fermata), or a word(s) (rondo form). See The "Concept Chart" on page 35.

• Mentor: This person helps a new music student become acquainted with the procedures and policies of the music room by assuming the role of "music buddy" or mentor. At the new student's first music lesson, the mentor student and the new student privately take some time to: complete the new student's Cumulative Musical Profile page (see pages 217-218), obtain a music book or new music folder, and reminds the teacher to add the new name to the seating chart and gradebook. During subsequent music lessons, the mentor may sit with the new student to assist with "catch up" learning.

• Row Managers (Roll-call Managers): These persons help organize individual rows of classmates for certain activities, including entering/exiting chairs in an acceptable manner. For very large student groups, such as elementary chorus, these persons take roll, and mark "row attendance" charts.

• Chair Squad: These persons set up/take down chairs for the music lesson. For the "music room on wheels," assign students to the Mobile Squad. These persons are scheduled throughout the day to transport the carts of instruments, turntable, tape player, records, tapes, student books, visual aids, and more from classroom to classroom within the school building.

• Music Books/Folder Managers: These persons pass out/collect all learning materials during the music lesson.

PERSONALIZING THE MUSIC ROOM

MORE NICKNAMES

Very young children love to personalize instruments, puppets and props used in the music lesson. When introducing classroom instruments, conduct the game, "Name the Baby." Invite children to think of names for the piano, autoharp, guitar, stereo, and more. Name suggestions are printed on slips of paper (by the grown-up at home, or the classroom teacher) and placed in the "music box" (a slotted box to hold all suggestions). After a designated time period, choose a name, and have a "coming out" party for the instrument. In one school, the piano was named "Melody," the guitar, "Gertrude," the autoharp, "Amos," and two fuzzy puppets, "Winky" and "Pinky." When a child thinks of handling an instrument like handling a baby, he/she may be more inclined to use care and a gentle touch.

A DIFFERENT REVEILLE

• Allow students to name the music room after an imaginary radio station. WMUS can become the headquarters for the morning "wake-up call." Each school day morning, just after the "Pledge of Allegiance" and before announcements, two older students play the selected music of the day over the P.A. system. Ahead of time, record favorite songs and instrumental pieces on cassette tape. In the morning, it is the student's job to get the tape player, cue the tape, and announce "Good morning, Central Elementary School. This is (student) and (student) bringing you the music of the day, titled (title of music)," and play it. Establish a schedule, so that all interested individuals have a turn sometime during the school year.

THE STARS ARE BORN

Budget appropriately for adequate financial resources and contract a "mobile recording unit" to come into the music room at the end of the school year to record each student music group singing their favorite songs. The tape of songs is then forwarded to a music company which specializes in mass-producing cassette tapes. Allow students to design the art for the cassette case. The end product: a cassette tape featuring music students as the "stars," available for all students and teachers as a memento of this year's musical activities.

PERSONALIZED STATIONERY

Each school year, invite all music students to design an illustration or logo which typifies their favorite part of music:

1) Be sure to instruct students to make black-line drawings only, as these reproduce well, and to include name and grade. Color illustrations reproduce as black-white images with varying shades of gray.

2) Designate a time period during which illustrations must be submitted.

3) Reduce each illustration, so that it comfortably occupies an area at the top of the stationery sheet. (Reducing the illustration refines the lines, and results in a clearer, more precise image.) Stationery can be reproduced on standard, 8 1/2" x 11" paper sheets, or on 4 1/4" x 5 1/2" sheets (using two illustrations, side-by-side on a standard sheet of paper, yielding two copies per sheet.)

4) Reproduce as many sheets of each illustration as desired.

5) Use the stationery for all school-related correspondence, and for student prizes. (With the assistance of the art or classroom teacher, these stationery sheets can be packaged up to make delightful gifts!)

LISTENING STATIONS

Establish listening stations in the music room. These are small cubicles of space which include a small table or desk, chair, tape player, headphones and an assortment of cassette tapes. Listening stations can also consist of a carpet square, large, overstuffed pillow, and tape player with headphones. A listening station is used for an individual listening experience, or as a "Time Away" place for a student requiring an alternate learning location. See section titled *Dealing With Inappropriate Behavior - the C.Y.B.* on page 22. Students love to personalize the listening stations with meaningful nicknames, such as: "Mars," "Space Station #289," and more.

A FORGOTTEN INVENTION

Pair students into partners, or invite them individually, to "invent" the "musical instrument that forgot to get invented." Students collaborate on the instrument's design and function, and draw and color an illustration of the instrument. Two criteria must be met:

1) The instrument must be complete with detailed parts such as valves, slides, mouthpieces, pedals, strings, mallets, electrical cables and so on.
2) The design of the instrument must be logically thought out, so that there is a "realistic" way for it to be held and played. The different "parts" of the instrument must work together to form the finished "whole."

The illustrations are titled, and shared for some imaginative, thought-provoking discussion. The illustrations can be collected and posted high on the walls as a personalized border around the music room.

THE MYSTERY TUNE

Keep a "mystery tune" posted in the music room at all times. Each month, student helpers post a new mystery tune on cards that sequence a familiar song. For example: train cars, racing cars, a chain of "paper dolls," planets in the solar system, a mother animal followed by baby animals, a parade of clowns, and more. Each car, animal, doll, planet or clown highlights a card on which is printed the rhythmic and/or melodic notation to the familiar song. Students are challenged to identify the music by its written notation. For extra credit, students can visit with you privately and identify the mystery tune by clapping the rhythm and/or playing the melody. Or, as a whole-group activity, the song can be clapped, played or sung, and individually identified for credit on separate slips of paper.

THE KIDS' KORNER

• This is the children's own bulletin board: MUSIC-MAKERS ARE NEWS MAKERS! Every month, select a different group of "music news managers" to research, compile, and post information about noteworthy musical events, famous musicians, up-coming musical happenings, and so on. But, the most important part of this bulletin board features the students' own musical news items. Keep everyone informed of student recitals, concerts, contests, honors and other recognitions. If Talent Day is approaching, publicize the date well in advance, so that student performers have ample time to rehearse their acts. See *A Talent Show* on page 91.

THE MUSIC ROOM PRINCIPLES

Post the Music Room Principles within easy view in the music room, perhaps on the inside of the door, so they are visible upon entering/exiting the music room. See *Music Room Principles: Choosing My Personal Power To Learn* on page 17.

THE NAME GAME

If music groups of early childhood learners come to music class only occasionally, or one lesson per week, it's often a challenge to remember their names. Design simple name tags which can be strung with yarn and worn around the neck, on which are printed each child's first name and the corresponding number of heartbeats or rhythm. For example:

Pau -la Jones

STUDENT EMPOWERMENT

When a music game or other activity demands its own set of personalized rules, empower your students to draw up their own. Then, the game meets THEIR standards, not YOURS. The game is owned and played by the students themselves.

SIMPLE ORGANIZERS

Obtain various, plastic "tubbies" (storage containers) and label each with the classroom teacher's name of each student group. Into these tubbies go student folders, "practice pages," music, and more. A simple, and efficient way to manage excessive amounts of paper.

11 BEYOND THE MUSIC ROOM

PUBLIC RELATIONS

Public Relations describes the relationship shared by the music teacher and ANYONE outside the music room. Effective public relations skills are often perceived as tantamount to the role of music educator since multitudes of individuals are affected by the school music program.

> "The music educator's power and responsibility to affect and influence children reaches far beyond the music room."

Figure that the typical elementary music educator teaches hundreds of children per week. These hundreds of children bring the music teacher together with parents, brothers and sisters, relatives, neighbors, friends and community members who attend music programs. These children also bring together the music teacher and their classroom teachers. Meetings which involve class scheduling bring the music teacher together with the instrumental, gym, art, library and computer teachers, and the principal and school secretary. Meetings which involve curriculum planning and evaluation bring the music teacher together with district administrators and fellow music educators.

Networking of this magnitude has obvious implications. The music educator's power and responsibility to affect and influence children merely begins in the music room, and potentially reaches far beyond the music room into the regular classroom, school, home and community. In other words, residual music teaching inadvertently happens.

Questions arise. When and where does the role of music teacher begin and end? Who exactly benefits from what goes on in the music room? The sensitive music teacher who addresses these thoughts and questions has already begun to develop his/her unique perception and style of "people skills." Following are descriptions of music-related activities which have been successful in promoting, maintaining or enhancing reciprocal, positive "public relationships." Determine the kinds of "musical" public relations activities that could bring together your unique style of music teaching and ANYONE outside your music room in the best possible way.

PUBLIC RELATIONS
WITHIN THE SCHOOL

A UNITED FRONT

Consider collaborating with the instrumental music teacher(s) on a mutual teaching goal. Together, brainstorm ideas for:

- Team-teaching units on sight-reading, ear-training, music composition, or memorization skills development.
- Team-teaching a unit on band and orchestra instruments.
- Sharing recognition of students' musical efforts.
- Sharing programs, demonstration classes, concerts and field trips.
- Sharing instrumental recruitment.
- Sharing publication of music newsletter.
- And others.

INTEGRATING MUSICAL CONCEPTS

Share the form, titled: "Collaborative-Teaching" on page 189 with classroom teachers. By choosing music materials which reinforce the classroom teacher's objectives (while first meeting the music teacher's!), the music teacher not only nurtures a professional relationship, but also invites the classroom teacher to learn more about music teaching. Almost all of the time, this shared approach to teaching meets a mutually satisfying goal: to broaden children's learning experiences.

> "By choosing music materials which reinforce the classroom teacher's objectives, the music teacher nurtures a professional relationship."

FINE ARTS MONTH

During the month of March, many schools become involved in Fine Arts Month which celebrates music, art and drama. In what ways can these departments unite in producing a multi-media educational experience for children which emphasizes the importance of the fine arts in the well-rounded development of the whole child?

Date: _____

Dear

Because Music Education offers our elementary school-aged children a broad spectrum of many diverse learning opportunities, perhaps an area of your classroom curriculum can be enhanced and reinforced through music instruction. If you are interested in collaborating musically on a selected unit of study, please complete the following brief questionnaire, and return it to me. Hopefully, by offering our children multiple perspectives from which to learn the same concepts, we can increase their learning awareness and capabilities, while at the same time, reach mutually satisfying teaching goals.

Musically yours,

_____

Music Teacher

(to be completed by collaborating teacher)

1) **SUBJECT AREA:** (for example: science, math, language, social studies, physical education, art, etc.)
_____

2) **SELECTED UNIT OF STUDY:** (for example: sound production, folk literature, a known historical period, famous persons, etc.)
_____

3) **ANTICIPATED COMPLETION OF SELECTED UNIT OF STUDY:** (date by which selected unit of study is to be completed)
_____

4) **BRIEF DESCRIPTION OF SELECTED UNIT OF STUDY:** (topics to be included)
_____
_____

(to be completed by music teacher, duplicated and shared)

1) **SUGGESTED MUSICAL REINFORCEMENT/ENRICHMENT ACTIVITIES:**
_____
_____

2) **DATE(S) OF COLLABORATIVE MUSIC INSTRUCTION:**
_____

(This page may be photocopied.)

LISTENING STATIONS

Might the school librarian entertain the thought of establishing "listening stations" in the library? Provided with tape recorders, headphones, and small cubicles of space, the librarian can "check out" a listening station to a child, just like checking out a book. Cassette tapes may be "checked out" from the music room, placed on loan to the library, or purchased for the school. Listening times can include regular library hours, before/after school, recess times and other times at the discretion of involved teachers.

MUSIC BOOK MARATHON

Identify the Dewey decimal, or Library of Congress numbers which identify music-related books in the school and community libraries. Publicize this number in the music room, so that students are aware of the sections in the library which contain music-related books. Now, as a reciprocal gesture to the librarian for setting up the listening stations, hold a Music Book Marathon for all students:

1) Designate a time period during which books may be read to qualify for an award, for example, the month of school which highlights "Book Week."
2) When a student has read a music-related book, he/she takes a book report form from the music teacher (or school office or classroom teacher) and fills it out. Very young children (Grades K-2) have a form which includes name, book title and a space for an illustration. Older children's book forms include title, author, and space for a brief description. See form on page 191.
3) The completed book report form is turned in to the music teacher who verifies the report by stamping or initialing it.
4) The stamped book report form is deposited in a box located in the student's classroom, which collects all book report forms for that class. The box is labelled with teacher's name (or the music group's musical nickname, for example: Ms. Aepler's Arpeggios).
5) At the conclusion of the designated time period, all stamped book report forms are collected. Multiple reports by the same student are stapled together.
6) The total number of books per participating student is tallied. The student who has read the largest number of books in his/her classroom, is noted. The student who has read the largest number of books in the entire school, is noted.

(top form — rotated)

Date: _____

Name: _____
Grade/Teacher: _____
Title of Book: _____

My drawing about this book:

MUSIC BOOK MARATHON

MUSIC BOOK MARATHON

Date: _____

Name: _____

Grade/Teacher: _____
Title of Book: _____
Author of Book: _____
Three things I learned from reading this book:
1) _____
_____
_____

2) _____
_____
_____

3) _____
_____
_____

MUSIC BOOK MARATHON

(Upper Elementary)

7) Students who have read the largest number of books in their class receive music awards such as musical pens, pencils, sharpeners, erasers, paper clips, bookmarks, pads of staff paper, tote bags or lollipops. The student who has read the largest number of books in the entire school receives a bigger prize such as gift-certificates to local music stores, tickets to local music events, music books or cassette tapes, records, T-shirts, etc. Check with the "boutique department" of local music stores and music mail-order catalogs for additional award ideas.

8) Remaining readers receive certificates of "honorable mention" for participation in the Music Book Marathon. See page 205.

SHOW-OFF

Can a request be made that the school's main bulletin board or showcase be reserved for the music department for a given period of time? Display photographs of children making music, as well as student work, information on upcoming musical events, stories or biographies of composers, musical symbols and terms, music from other lands, and more.

KEEPING THE BALL ROLLING

Invite classroom teachers to share your current musical objectives. Distribute trendy "practice pages" that reinforce musical concepts which you are currently teaching. Classroom teachers can encourage students to complete these during indoor recess or free time. A student who turns in a "practice page" to the music teacher receives extra credit toward his/her music evaluation.

▶ "A sensitive music educator asks for support from the building principal by first giving it."

YOU'RE INVITED

Invite classroom teachers to share the last five minutes of music class to observe or participate in the closing activity. Even if a classroom teacher is unavailable, the mere invitation suggests a high regard for that individual in the music room.

THE GOLDEN RULE

Within the printed program of a musical concert, or aloud at a musical assembly, introduce the building principal to the audience, and mention the specific ways in which this individual contributes to children's musical growth through his/her support of the music program. Musical events typically draw more people to the elementary school than other activities, excluding voting. This individual, whom the music teacher counts on for support, is also in need of support from his/her staff and parent group. In other words, a sensitive music educator asks for support by first giving it.

MUTUAL SUPPORT

All educators want and need to feel the support of the building principal and other supervisory individuals. For music educators, the principal often offers "support" in the very best way that he/she knows. And yet, because of differing perceptions of what support IS, the music educator may perceive a lack of support. Here is a simple tactic which helps the principal and teacher identify their mutual needs for support in concrete terms. The music teacher presents to the principal a written list of three to five specific ways in which the principal could best satisfy the music teacher's "support requirements" for the music program. For example:

1) Become thoroughly acquainted with the music teacher's method of discipline, and be available for appropriate follow-through measures.
2) Make at least two active visitations to the music room during which the principal takes part in musical activities with the students, and models interest and enthusiasm for music.
3) Open school music programs with a brief introduction of the music teacher(s), and an acknowledgement of the benefits of music education to all children.

Now for the important part: along with this written list of the music teacher's "support requirements" is a second list which the principal identifies as his/her list of "support requirements" as needed from the music teacher. It is both fair and logical that principal and music educator be reciprocal in stating their individual needs for support. This approach promotes empathy and greater understanding of one another's perceptions of support, and fosters continued, effective communication.

> **"It is both fair and logical that principal and music educator be reciprocal in stating their individual needs for support."**

CONGRATULATIONS!

When appropriate, send home notes and/or photos of music students who are recognized for achievements: musical, behavioral, effort, and more. A small note of congratulations personalizes the correspondence. (See stationery in Chapter 12.)

X-TRA! X-TRA! READ ALL ABOUT IT

Publicize musical happenings within the school, or school-related musical happenings in the community by inviting local newspaper(s) to cover the event(s). Arrange a date for a photo, and forward all pertinent information about the event including who, what, where, when and how, to the editor, at least four weeks in advance of the event. Double-check for accurate spellings of children's names who are pictured in the photo and/or article.

FREE PRESS

Three to six times per school year, select a group of students who collaborate with the music teacher to publish the school music newsletter, THE MUSIC NOTE. Research instruments, composers, musical events, students musical honors, musical riddles and anecdotes and compile, edit and arrange information. Specify dates and times for publication meetings, and have these posted outside the music room. During meetings, play a selected musical recording and use this time to briefly highlight a specific musical concept or composer. Select a different group of music students from different classes for each publication, so that many children participate. Circulate THE MUSIC NOTE to parents, administrators, classroom teachers, district music teachers, local, private music teachers, and other "teachable clientele."

> ▷ **"Circulate THE MUSIC NOTE to parents, administrators, classroom teachers, district music teachers, local, private music teachers, and other 'teachable clientele.'"**

HELP WANTED

Advertise in THE MUSIC NOTE for parent and/or community helpers who could provide services for musical activities such as: sewing, building, chaperoning, supervising, driving, cooking, organizing, telephoning, corresponding, and more. Parents are often eager to provide an integral service to the music program, and they enjoy being remembered with a note of thanks from the music teacher and students.

PUBLIC RELATIONS
OUTSIDE THE SCHOOL

A GOLDRUSH

Within many communities there is a "gold mine" of talented, resourceful, musically-inclined individuals who bring fresh new perspectives to the music lesson. Give some thought to inviting a community member to share his/her musical expertise with a group of students, and award this individual with a Tune-a-Gram (on page 203) and "thank you" card signed by members of the music class. This person typically becomes a supportive comrade, and allies him/herself to the goodness of music education within the community.

> ▶ **"When a student performer receives applause and a certificate of participation, his/her personal and musical achievement is celebrated not only by peers, but by very significant grown-ups as well."**

DIAL-A-MUSIC TEACHER

Compile a list of local, private music teachers who give permission to have their names, addresses and telephone numbers circulated to interested parents. In addition to the list of private teachers, include a page of questions which parents can ask to help determine the best teacher to meet their child's musical needs. See form on p. 196.

TALENT DAY

Refer to *A Talent Show* on page 91, for a description of a mini-talent show held in the music room during a regularly-scheduled music class. With students' majority consent, invite classroom teachers, building principal, and especially parents to share students' performances. When a student performer receives applause and a certificate of participation, his/her personal and musical achievement is celebrated not only by peers, but by very significant grown-ups as well.

DEAR PARENT:

Choosing a private music teacher for your child is one of the most important decisions you will make. In order to help you in your selection process, here are a number of questions to ask each individual teacher, along with an attached list of local teachers in our community.
Sincerely,

_____

Music Teacher

1) From what musical institution did you receive your music education?

2) How long have you been teaching music?

3) Describe the goals you have set for your private students.

4) To what professional organizations do you belong?

5) What is the recommended student age for beginning private lessons?

6) To what method of teaching do you subscribe? What methods might I as a parent note, in the form of books, supplementary materials, theory courses, etc.?

7) Do you present recitals? What other performance opportunities are your students exposed to? Do you enter your students in contests or competitions?

8) How much daily practice time do you request of your students?

9) What are some ways in which I can encourage consistent practice habits at home?

10) How long is the music lesson?

11) What is the fee per music lesson?

12) What other expenses should I be aware of in addition to books, materials, contest fees, etc?

13) What kind of payment plan do you offer?

14) Can missed lessons be made up? Is there a penalty for missed lessons?

15) Is there any other information regarding your music studio that I should know about?

16) May I please request two references from parents whose children have studied with you for at least five years?

(This page may be photocopied.)

BIAL-A-MUSIC TEACHER

RESOURCE FILE – LOCAL MUSIC TEACHERS

(Private Music Teachers and/or Studios)

Name	Address	Phone	Type of Instruction

THE UN-CONCERT

Entertain the idea of a "music demonstration class." This is not a recital, program, concert or anything of the like. When the music teacher finds him/herself short on time, or "concerted out" due to too many performances, and is in need of a performance opportunity for a group of students, here is an option. Inform the students that during an up-coming, regularly-scheduled music lesson, parents will be invited to attend the music class. Plan the music lesson as usual, only include some activities which invite parental participation. For example: a movement sequence which students could teach to mom or dad, or an instrumental activity in which he/she could play a classroom instrument. This type of musical experience is not only entertaining, but informative and educational as well. While sharing the joy of music-making with his/her child, a parent gains a new musical perspective from two viewpoints:

1) Being the learner in music class along with child.
2) Being the observer, noting short-term learning outcomes, and immediate benefits of music education for children.

STAR-STRUCK

Why not stage a non-competitive, all-school Talent Show? Consider a non-audition format, in which all would-be performers are automatically accepted into the show, providing the act meets certain qualifications or guidelines of musical and ethical taste. Ask for assistance from the Parent Teacher Organization. Establish a Talent Show Committee, which include parents, teachers and the building principal, as consultant.

1) Publicize dates for both the Preview and the Talent Show.
2) List performance qualifications or guidelines. Acts not meeting these requirements are subject to revision and/or cancellation at the discretion of the Talent Show Committee.
3) Post a sign-up sheet in every classroom, and faculty lounge. (School staff can get in on the act, too!) Include student and/or parent names and telephone numbers. Highlight a DEADLINE DATE for sign-up. Highlight the PREVIEW DATE.
4) Categorize all acts according to age, theme or complexity. List the acts, including student names and phone numbers.
5) All acts must report to the Preview or be subject to cancellation. The Preview should be scheduled within two weeks of the actual Talent Show. It is conducted in the same performance room (stage?) as the Talent Show. Each act is performed and reviewed by the Talent Show Committee. Recommendations are made for improvement regarding volume, stage presence, expression, style, bow, entrance and exit, and so on.

6) A musical opener, such as an arrangement of *Hooray For Hollywood* or *There's No Business Like Show Business*, is played to accompany the introduction of all Talent Show performers at the beginning of the show. A very simple line-up (according to height) can be rehearsed at the beginning or end of the Preview.

7) Specific roles are assigned, such as: Mistress/Master of Ceremonies, "green room" supervisors, audio technician, lighting technician, awards manager, program manager, and publication manager, among others.

8) Performers are directed to bring all costumes, make-up, and props to a designated place before the Talent Show. Performers meet in a designated place on the day of the Talent Show. Changing rooms are labeled and available.

9) After the Talent Show, all performers and persons performing other roles as listed in #7 are presented with certificates of participation, as well as ribbons or buttons proclaiming: Super Star!

10) The goal of the Talent Show may be to produce a musically entertaining and educational event in and of itself, or it can be staged to meet another goal: to raise money for a school project.

HONORARY GRANDPARENTS

Looking for an audience for the dress rehearsal of a children's music program? What about inviting a local senior citizens group into the school to act as the "preview audience"? An audience sparks an emotional fervor in performers which boosts their performance awareness and capabilities, and gives the dress rehearsal the flavor of a true performance. Seniors are grateful to be around children and be entertained at the same time. Request the aid of the building custodian(s) when arranging for comfortable seating, wheelchair access, and the like.

> "An audience sparks an emotional fervor in performers which boosts their performance awareness and capabilities."

MUSICAL PEN PALS

Encourage music classes to communicate with music groups from other schools by forming "musical pen pals." Each month or so, students correspond with one another about music class, chorus activities, etc. Students write their thoughts on one, collective group letter. Share the letters in music class. Chorus groups can culminate the year of communication with shared, exchange concerts. Each group performs a designated number of songs, and both groups perform a combined number. Children can learn through real-life experiences that music is a great communicator, and that music bonds people together.

FAN MAIL

Encourage students to write to their favorite musical heroes/heroines. Research names and addresses. Share any correspondence in music class.

ON THE ROAD

Invite parents and other teachers to chaperone a field trip to:

- The symphony.
- A recording studio.
- A local theatre production.
- A local choral performance.
- A music publishing company.
- Engage in a performance at the local shopping mall or senior citizens center.

WIDE-ANGLE LENS

Collaborate with district music teachers about the possibility of a district-wide music festival. Target a specific age group of student participants. If desired, seek guest composers/arrangers for commissioned pieces of music, and/or guest conductors. Make contact early, at least one year in advance. Arrange for budgeting of music, supplies, guest artist fees, music hall rental, sound technicians, recording technicians, videographer, printed programs, and more. Allow at least one year in advance of the festival to plan and prepare. Delegate all efforts and responsibilities to well-organized committees. A great deal of time and effort typically proves to be one of the most outstanding and memorable musical experiences ever achieved by a group of children united by their teachers through the love of music.

ARTISTS IN RESIDENCE

An exceptional educational opportunity! Research available funds (grants, foundations) which could support the "live-in" arrangement of a highly-specialized master teacher, conductor, song-writer, or performer. This individual(s) "resides" at the school for a given period of time, usually a school quarter or semester, and is continually "on-call" to teach, demonstrate, evaluate, and provide hands-on experiences in his/her area of musical expertise. An unequalled learning experience for students and educators, alike!

12 AWARDS, DOCUMENTS
FORMS, AND MORE

Make each minute of your valuable teaching time count by doing what you do best – teaching! The following forms, and others throughout this book bring teaching efficiency to your fingertips. You'll find an organized collection of reproducible sheets which have been designed to meet many of your classroom needs.

The Very Special Person Award

This is to Certify that

_____

has earned a Tune-A-Gram for

_____

on

_____

_____   _____
_____   _____
_____   _____

The Very Special Person Award

This is to Certify that

_____

has earned a Tune-A-Gram for

_____

on

_____

_____   _____
_____   _____
_____   _____

MUSIC AWARD

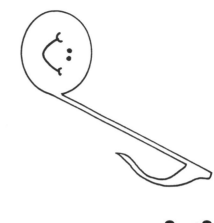

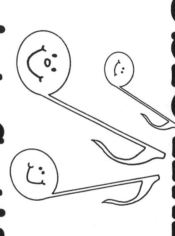

This is to Certify That

_____

Has participated in Musical Activities
of the

_____

at _____

Date _____

Music Award

This is to Certify That

Has participated in Musical Activities of the

_____

at _____

Date _____

Cut out circles, place on ribbon
and photocopy to create different awards.

Sound Off. . .

Music Students Really

MEASURE UP

Chorus Members . . .

Hal-le - lu -jah

Handel

. . . are something to sing about

Please Take Note

LETTER OF COMMUNICATION (SAMPLE FORMAT)

By keeping the language as "musical" as possible, written communications (to parents, staff members, administrators, can not only be informative, but clever and fun to read as well! For example:

CENTRAL ELEMENTARY SCHOOL   SEPTEMBER 7,

PLEASE TAKE NOTE!

Greetings from the Central Elementary Music Room where eager, young *vocalists* and *instrumentalists* diligently pra their music. We'd like to say "Welcome aboard" to our new musicians, and "Welcome *Bach*" to our many seasc musicians! This year, all students seem to be in *fine form,* and on a *scale* of 1 to 10, the enthusiasm rates at least 11 - *introduction* to a great year *fa* all of us!

OTHER MUSICALLY ADAPTABLE WORDS AND/OR PHRASES:

- Here is a *Liszt* of some upcoming events . . .

- The music program features some *major* points, and some *minor* ones, too . . .

- *Step* in and visit our classes . . .

- See how our *key* musicians *measure* up and *Handel* their music . . .

- It's no *treble* to inform you of some of our music program's *bassic* facts . . .

- Students *pitch* in to make our Chorus great . . .

- The school musical *drums* up a lot of business within our community . . .

- *Chordially* yours, The Music Director

Use your own creative imagination to *improvise* more catchy, musical quips!

MUSIC PLANNING CALENDAR

At–a–glance" overview of holidays, seasons and special occasion days for use in planning programs, concerts, assemblies nd supplementary units of study throughout the school year)

EPTEMBER Open House _____
PTA/PTO Assembly _____
Other _____

CTOBER Hot Lunch Week _____
Columbus Day, Oct. 14 _____
United Nations Day, Oct. 24 _____
Halloween, Oct. 31 _____
Other _____

OVEMBER Veterans Day, Nov. 11 _____
American Education Week _____
Book Week _____
Thanksgiving _____
Other _____

ECEMBER Chanukah season _____
Human Rights Day, Dec. 10 _____
Bill of Rights Day, Dec. 15 _____
Christmas, Dec. 25 _____
Other _____

ANUARY Martin Luther King Jr. Day, Jan. 19 _____
National Teacher Appreciation Day, Jan. 28 _____
Other _____

EBRUARY Afro–American History Month _____
Abraham Lincoln's Birthday, Feb. 12 _____
Valentine's Day, Feb. 14 _____
George Washington's Birthday, Feb. 18 _____
Brotherhood Week _____
Other _____

ARCH MUSIC IN OUR SCHOOLS MONTH _____
Youth Art Month _____
St. Patrick's Day, March 17 _____
Other _____

PRIL National Library Week _____
National Secretaries Day _____
Arbor Day, April 30 _____
Easter/Passover season _____
Other _____

AY Spring Performance/Musical/Talent Show _____
Mother's Day _____
Other _____

UNE Flag Day, June 14 _____
Father's Day _____
Other _____

DAILY TEACHING SCHEDULE

SCHOOL: _____ SEMESTER: _____

MUSIC DIRECTOR: _____

TIME	MONDAY	TUESDAY	WEDNESDAY	THURSDAY	FRIDAY

MUSICAL THEMES FOR BULLETIN BOARDS

_____ WHO'S WHO – "Music Makers are Newsmakers"...
Examples: known composers, playwrights, performers, producers, etc.

_____ SEASONS AND HOLIDAYS – "Spring Sing"...
Examples: Thanksgiving, Valentine's Day, springtime, etc.

_____ MUSIC VOCABULARY – "Let's Come to TERMS"...
Examples: crescendo, allegro, molto ritardando, etc.

_____ PROGRAM ANNOUNCEMENTS – "On with the Show!"...
Examples: musical program dates, times, places and photographs of student performers, etc.

_____ DISPLAYS OF STUDENT WORK – "NOTEworthy Students"...
Examples: theory assignments, music dictation, original compositions, etc.

_____ CAREERS IN MUSIC – C horeographer
                          A rranger
                          R ecord producer
                          E lectric guitarist
                          E ngineer in recording studio
                          R adio disc jockey
                          S inger

_____ INSTRUMENTS – "Instrument Family Tree"...
Examples: families of instruments (old and new), ethnic instruments, home-made instruments, etc.

_____ MUSICAL STYLES – "Music Lives On through Time"...
Examples: jazz, pop, classical, rock, country, blues, ragtime, electronic, etc.

_____ MUSICAL ELEMENTS – "The Ingredients of Music"...
Examples: rhythm, melody, harmony, form, tempo, dynamics, tone color, style, etc.

_____ OTHER IDEAS –

VOCAL AUDITION GUIDE

NAME:_____ GRADE:_____ DATE:_____

SCHOOL:_____ MUSIC DIRECTOR:_____

1. VOCAL RANGE

Soprano   Alto   Baritone (changing voice)

2. VOCAL QUALITY

Focused (pure, clear)

Bright (thin)

Dark (thick)

Nasal (pinched, reedy)

Airy (breathy)

Husky (raspy)

Driven (strident)

Comments: _____

3. VOCAL RESONANCE

Tone rings with full head resonance

Tone is somewhat resonant

Tone is inhibited, throaty – needs practice

Comments: _____

4. BREATH SUPPORT

Tone projects with support and energy

Tone is somewhat supported

Tone lacks support -- needs practice

Comments: _____

5. FLEXIBILITY

Tone is free (vocal passages are sung with ease

    throughout the vocal range)

Tone is somewhat flexible

Tone is strained (difficulty singing freely) – needs practice

Comments: _____

6. PITCH AWARENESS – SINGS IN TUNE

All of the time

Most of the time

Some of the time

None of the time

Comments: _____

7. ENUNCIATION

Sings with open vowel sounds

Vowel sounds are somewhat open

Experiences difficulty in forming open vowel sounds

    (rigid jaw) – needs practice

Comments: _____

8. DICTION

Consonants are articulate, clear

Consonants are somewhat articulate

Consonants are undefined – needs practice

Comments: _____

9. DYNAMIC RANGE

Sings with musically appropriate louds and softs

Sings with developing dynamic contrasts

Needs practice to develop dynamic contrasts

Comments: _____

10. STAGE PRESENCE

Performance is poised and confident

Performance shows developing confidence

Performance lacks confidence –

    needs practice and experience

Comments: _____

ADDITIONAL COMMENTS:

_____

_____

_____

_____

_____

_____

_____

_____

_____

_____

_____

_____

_____

MUSIC PERFORMANCE PLANNING GUIDE – SONG SELECTION

A "theme" can pull a program of songs together by creating an overall mood for the performance. In addition, a program's musical content can be balanced and educationally sound, as well as entertaining, by selecting songs from the following list:

_____ An "opener" or a rousing, spirited welcoming-type song (perhaps the school song) or a song which introduces the theme of the program.

_____ A choreographed song(s) with body motions or dance steps.

_____ A vocally challenging song(s) which features two-or three-part harmony with canon, partner-songs or counter-melodies.

_____ A song(s) which features instrumental accompaniments on rhythm instruments (hand drums, maracas, tambourines, etc.) or pitched melody or harmony instruments (guitar, autoharp, bells, metallophones, xylophones, etc.)

_____ A patriotic song(s).

_____ A song(s) which typifies an era such as: the turn of the century, '20s, '30s, '40s, '50s, etc.

_____ A seasonal song(s).

_____ A ballad or slow-tempo, emotionally exciting song(s).

_____ A silly, frivolous, nonsense song(s) just for fun.

_____ A "pop" style song.

_____ A song(s) which features the special talents of individual students.

_____ An audience participation or "sing-along" song.

_____ A choral reading or spoken musical piece.

_____ A "closer" which relates to the theme and unifies the program's selections while creating a strong, unforgettable impact at the program's conclusion.

IT'S SHOWTIME!

🎼 Mark your calendars! The date is set! Our musical program:

_____

will be performed for you on _____

at _____ o'clock, at _____

Featured performers are members of the

_____

Won't you please come and share this special musical performance with us?

We're looking forward to seeing you!

Musically yours,

_____

and the

_____

STAFF COMMUNICATION LETTER

Dear Staff:

The _____ is eagerly and diligently

group

practicing for their upcoming musical performance:

_____ to be held on _____

name of program   date

at _____ at (or in) _____

        time   place or room

The program will be performed for you on _____

                                            date

at _____ .

        time

Due to the musical rehearsals which take place prior to this performance, our routine teaching schedules are somewhat affected. Every effort is being made to keep schedule changes to a minimum, while at the same time affording our performers ample preparation time to ensure a well-rehearsed and musically exciting program for all.

Please note the rehearsal times listed below, and adjust your schedules accordingly. It is hoped that any schedule change is only a slight inconvenience for you. If there is anything I can do to help solve any significant schedule conflicts, please let me know immediately.

Thank you very much for your cooperation, patience and flexibility. Your support of our music program and encouragement for our student musicians are recognized and greatly appreciated!

Thanks from the Music Room,

_____

Music Director

REHEARSAL: _____

                  date

_____

                  time

_____

                  place

SCHOOL PERFORMANCE: _____

      date

_____

time

_____

place

REHEARSAL: _____

                  date

_____

                  time

_____

                  place

PARENT PERFORMANCE: _____

date

_____

time

_____

place

PARENT PERMISSION SLIP

Dear Music Parent:

The _____ has been invited to

group

perform for the _____

event

at _____ on _____

place   date

Please indicate permission for your child's attendance by completing the permission slip below.

It must be returned to school by _____ .

date

Thank you for your cooperation.

_____

Music Director

- - - ✂ -

_____ has my permission to perform

student's name

for _____ at _____

event   place

on _____ .

_____

Parent or Guardian

STUDENT CUMULATIVE MUSICAL PROFILE – LOWER ELEMENTARY

NAME: _____ DATE: _____ AGE: _____

SCHOOL: _____ MUSIC DIRECTOR: _____

HOME ADDRESS: _____
                                          street

_____
        city   state   zip

PHONE: _____

PARENT OR GUARDIAN: _____

1. MUSIC CLASS IN SCHOOL

Lessons per Week: 1   2   3   4   5   Minutes per Lesson: _____

2. PRIVATE OR GROUP LESSONS (Outside of School)

Piano   Violin   Dance   Drama   Voice   Guitar   Other: _____

Lessons per Week: 1   2   3   4   5

Private Teacher's Name or Name of Studio: _____

Length of Study: _____ Number of Performances per Year: _____

Solo: _____

3. OTHER PERFORMING ARTS INVOLVEMENT (Outside of School)

Church Chorus   Children's Theater   Other: _____

Name of Group: _____

Number of Performances per Year: _____

Solo: _____

4. PROGRAM/CONCERT ATTENDANCE

Musical Programs Attended Within the Last Year:

_____   _____

_____   _____

_____   _____

5. STUDENT'S FAVORITE MUSICAL INSTRUMENT(S): _____

6. STUDENT'S FAVORITE MUSICAL ACTIVITY: _____

7. COMMENTS: _____

_____

_____

_____

_____

_____

_____

_____

_____

_____

_____

STUDENT CUMULATIVE MUSICAL PROFILE – UPPER ELEMENTARY

NAME: _____ DATE: _____ AGE: _____

SCHOOL: _____ MUSIC DIRECTOR: _____

HOME ADDRESS: _____
street

_____
| | | |
city   state   zip

PHONE: _____

PARENT OR GUARDIAN: _____

1. MUSIC CLASS IN SCHOOL

   Lessons per Week: 1 2 3 4 5   Minutes per Lesson: _____

2. SCHOOL PERFORMING GROUP

   Chorus   Band   Orchestra

                             Instrument: Instrument:

                             _____   _____

   Other Performing Groups: _____

3. PRIVATE OR GROUP LESSONS (Outside of School)

   Piano   Violin   Dance   Drama   Voice   Guitar   Other: _____

   Lessons per Week: 1   2   3   4   5

   Private Teacher's Name or Name of Studio: _____

   Length of Study: _____ Number of Performances per Year: _____

   Solo: _____

4. OTHER PERFORMING ARTS INVOLVEMENT (Outside of School)

   Church Chorus   Children's Theater   Other: _____

   Name of Group: _____

   Number of Performances per Year: _____

   Solo: _____

5. PROGRAM/CONCERT ATTENDANCE

   Musical Programs Attended Within the Last Year:

   _____   _____

   _____   _____

   _____   _____

6. STUDENT'S FAVORITE MUSICAL INSTRUMENT(S): _____

7. STUDENT'S FAVORITE MUSICAL ACTIVITY: _____

8. COMMENTS: _____

   _____

   _____

   _____

   _____

NEWS BULLETIN

DATE: _____

SCHOOL: _____

ADDRESS: _____

PHONE: _____

MUSIC DIRECTOR: _____

Who:

What:

Where:

When:

How:

CURRICULUM GOALS SUMMARY

GRADE: _____   YEAR: _____

SONGS, GAMES, ACTIVITIES	CONCEPTS	SKILLS

INDEX

A

Artwork, 8
Assessment
    Assessment of Musical Learning Outcomes
        form, 161
    earned points, 157-158
    Musical Learning Outcomes form, 160
    non-assessment, 159
    observable music skills, 156-157
    self-assessment, 159
    Shared Assessment of Musical Learning
        Outcomes form, 162
Atmosphere in the music class,
    artwork, 8
    birthdays, 11
    child's individual learning potential, 4
    child's personal learning power, 3
    child's self concept as a predicter of learning
        success, 3
    children's strong points, recognizing, 4
    competition vs. collaboration, 4
    constructive criticism, 9, 11
    disappointment, dealing with, 99
    evaluation of classroom atmosphere, 1
    get-well wishes, 11
    humor, 13-14
    invite children's participation, 9, 103
    learning noise, 7
    musical nicknames, 6
    philosophy for lesson planning, 3
    positive reinforcers, 7
    positive teaching attitude, 2
    practice pages vs. worksheets, 103
    process vs. product, 4
    school song, 13
    sing-along, 102
    teacher's attitude, 1
    tune-a-grams, 13, 202
    uniqueness of each individual, 5
    weather, when students complain about, 102
    when a class is late, 5
    word choice, 9
    See also *Self concept*
Attention grabbers
    alarm clocks, 94
    using jokes to establish pitch, 108
Attitude warm-ups
    winning attitude check-list, 122
    young children, 122
Awards
    Create Award, 101
    individual awards, 21
    most improved award, 21
    popcorn party, 106
    stickers, 21

B

Beat, strategies for teaching
    beat notation, 40
    beatnik, the, 39, 125
    differences between beat and rhythm, 144-145
    internalizing, 39-40
    ways to show, 39
Big Belly Breath, 128

B (Birthdays)

Birthdays
    composers, 88
    students, 11
Breathing warm-ups
    balloon, to demonstrate breathing, 127
    Big Belly Breath, 128
    describing the breathing process, 127
    feather, to demonstrate breathing, 127
    performance anxiety, 128
    songs, 129
    verbal analogies, 129
    wind chimes, to demonstrate, breathing, 128

C

Calypso Birthday Party, A, 12
Check Your Behavior – the C.Y.B., 22
    C.Y.B. reminder, 22
    consequences, 22
    failure to comply with written assignment, 25
    mini-conference, 23
    musi-contract, 25-27
    phone call to parent/guardian, 24
    second violation, 22
    subsequent music lesson, 23
    teacher empathy, 24
    time away place, 22
    See also *Inappropriate behavior*
Choreography, *See Movement and Direction*
Class rules, 16-18
    categories, 17
    examples, 17
Classroom Management
    appropriate behavior, acknowledging, 18
    appropriate behavior, examples, 20
    class rules, 16, 185
    manners, teaching, 102
    principles for developing a system, 16
    rewarding specific behavior, 18-19
    simple behavior interventions, 28-29, 89
    taking turns, 108
    whole-group behavior management, 19-21
    See also *Inappropriate behavior*
Closing
    adapting lyrics of a song, 116
    reinforcing newly-learned concepts, 118
    time fillers, 117-119
    various languages, 116
Composers
    birthdays, 88
    introducing, 87
    See also *Music listening*
Cooperative learning groups
    melody, teaching strategies, 65-66
    naming groups, 103
    talking out of turn, 94
Criticism, constructive, 9, 11

D

Direction, *See Movement and Direction*
Discipline
    class rules, 16-18
    climate for learning, 15
    principles for developing a system, 16
    teacher/student roles, 16
    unfavorable conditions, 15
Dynamics, strategies for teaching
    clapping, 104

(continued)

    flash cards, 73
    games, 73-74
    movement, 75
    pianoforte, history, 75-76
    posters, 74
    singing, 76
    tape recorder, 76
    visual relationship, 75

E

Effective music teaching
    conditions of, 2
    products of, 155
    negative learning outcomes, 163-165
    results, 155
Evaluation
    examples, 153
    failure to achieve learning outcomes, 163-165
    frequency of evaluation periods, 153
    games, 97
    individual assessment, 152
    information to be gained from, 151
    learning-challenged children, 154
    observable music skills, 156-157
    relationship between teacher's skills and
        learning outcomes, 151
    self concept related to evaluation, 153
    self-referenced norms vs. group reference
        norms, 155
    whole-group evaluation, 101, 165-177
    See also *Assessment*

F

Flash cards
    dynamics, 73, 76
    form, 83
    melody, 64-65, 145
    movement, 81
    rhythm, 47, 50, 145
Form, strategies for teaching
    flash cards, 83
    music "maps," 82
    rondo form, 83
    sound sheets, 83

G

Greeting
    adapting lyrics of a song, 112
    bean bag, 116
    seasonal songs, 113
    various languages, 111

H

Harmony, strategies for teaching
    chanting in canon, 67
    chords, introducing with autoharp, 69
    ear training, 69
    major and minor, 69
    movement, 68
    partner songs, 68
    tape recorder, in teaching harmony, 68
Hello, *See Greeting*
Humor in the classroom, 13-14

I

Inappropriate behavior
    C.Y.B. ("Check Your Behavior"), 22
    C.Y.B. reminder, 22
    consequences, 22
    failure to comply with written assignment, 25
    mini-conference, 23
    musi-contract, 25-27
    phone call to parent/guardian, 24
    second violation, 22
    simple behavior interventions, 28-29
    subsequent music lesson, 23
    teacher empathy, 24
    time-away place, 22
Interpretive symbols and terms, strategies for
    teaching
    games, 84-85
    introducing, 83
    memorizing, 86
    reinforcement, 90
    visualization, 84
Inner ear, developing, 63, 69,145, 147

L

Learning process
    examples, 32
    long range view, 31
Lesson plan, *See Music Lesson*

M

Melody, strategies for teaching
    commercials, 66
    cooperative learning, 65-66
    ear training, 63
    echo singing, 62-63
    flash cards, 65
    games, 60, 64-65
    high and low, 59
    lip-sync to recordings, 67
    matching pitch, 62, 107
    music listening, 67
    music staff, introducing, 60, 92
    mystery tune, 184
    new pitch, introducing a, 63
    notation, 54, 103
    note names, 105
    ostinato, 148
    physical response, 60
    piano, 105
    portable keyboards, 66
    practice pages, 57-58
    scale, using to teach melody, 62
    sound maps, 61
    visual relationship of pitches, 62
Meter, strategies for teaching
    bouncing balls, 56
    conducting patterns, 56
    games, 53-54
    games, 57
    introducing, 50
    Meter Bingo, 57
    meter jives, 51-55
Mini-conference, 23
More We Get Together, The, 112
Motor warm-ups
    aerobic warm-ups, 124

beat jive activities, 123-124
    stretching, 125
    young children, 125
Movement and Direction, strategies for teaching
    choosing partners, 99
    clockwise/counterclockwise, 110
    dance steps, teaching, 83
    echoing, 81
    flash cards, 81
    gross motor movement, 95
    learning challenged students, 82
    mirror, using to teach movement, 96
    mirroring, 81
    new song, learning with movement, 146
    right and left, 110
    shadowing, 81
    using a compass, 109
    warm-ups, 81
Musi-contract
    conference, 26
    implementation, 26
    incentive, 26
    purpose, 25
    reproducible form, 27
    when to use, 25
    See also *Inappropriate behavior*
Musi-Quest, 165-170
Music Folder
    sticker awards, 21
    preparation, 37
Music lesson
    concept chart, 35
    lesson plan format, 33
    menu, comparing lesson to, 91
    partners teaching partners, 36
    philosophy, 3
    questioning strategies, 35
    reproducible form, 34
    teacher talk, 35
    whole group instruction, 35
    whole group movement, 35
Music listening
    listening leagues, 99
    listening stations, 183
    melody, strategies for teaching, 67
    music maps, 82
    rhythm, strategies for teaching, 44
    sound sheets, 83
Music Map, A, 82
Musical Place Settings, 79
Music Round Robin, 171-175
Music-Tac-Toe, 175-177

N

New Songs
    books and pictures, 140
    introducing, 139-140
    memorizing, 148-149
    musical concept, emphasizing, 146
    practicing, 144-149
    props, 139
    questions to ask, 141
    rhythm canons, 147
    short story, 140
    teaching the song, 140
    transferring previously learned concepts, 141-142
    Twenty Guidelines, 142-144
    using movement to teach, 146

young or special-needs children, 142-144

O

Ostinato,
    melody, 148
    rhythm, 148
Outcome-based learning
    definition, 32
    goals, 32
    process, 32
Organization
    alphabetizing students by name, 100
    music box, 96
    plastic tubbies, 96, 185
    seating charts, 101
    student jobs and responsibilities, 180-182

P

Partner songs, 68
Performance
    performance anxiety, 101, 128
    risers, arranging students, 92
    watching the director, 94
Personalizing the music class
    imaginary instruments, 184
    listening stations, 183
    making a recording, 183
    music bulletin board, 184
    music room "radio station," 182
    music stationery, 183
    ownership of the music experience, 179-180
    personalizing games, 185
    poster of last year's classes, 111
    student jobs and responsibilities, 180-182
    video of last year's classes, 111
Phrase, strategies for teaching
    learning songs, 96
    movement, 59
    relating to the breath, 58
Pitch, *See Melody*
Pop Bottle Symphony, 79
Posture warm-ups
    demonstrating, 126
    games, 126
    mental imagery, 126
Power thoughts, 33
Practice pages, 103
Project Create, 36
Props
    balloon, to teach breathing, 127
    compass, to teach movement and direction, 109
    feather, to teach breathing, 127
    gift box, 114
    hula hoops to teach gross motor movement, 95
    hula hoops with rhythm instruments, 95
    introducing new songs, 139
    metronome, to teach tempo, 114
    mirror, to teach movement and singing, 96
    nicknames, 182
    stuffed animals to coax shy students, 94
    toy microphones for echo activities, 93
    walkie talkies for echo activities, 93
    wind chimes, to teach breathing, 127
    wind-up toys to teach tempo, 93
Public relations
    artists in residence, 201
    classroom teacher, 188, 192

collaborative teaching form, 189
definition, 187
field trips, 200
fine arts month, 188
guest speakers from the community, 195
instrumental music teacher, 188
library, 190
local newspaper, 194
Music Book Marathon, 190-192
music festival, 200
musical pen pals, 200
parents, 193
performances, 198
principal, 192-193
private music teacher, 195-197
school bulletin board, 192
school music newspaper, 194
senior citizens, 199
writing to musical celebrities, 200

R

Reproducible forms, 201
Rhythm, strategies for teaching
    canons, 147
    difference between beat and rhythm, 41, 144-145
    echo clapping, 41-42
    flash cards, 47, 50
    games, 46-50
    learning to spell, 105
    memory, 41, 50
    music listening, 44
    music notes for keeping score in games, 106
    ostinato, 48, 148
    reading rhythms, 43, 145, 148
    rhythm instruments, 42
    Rockin' Body Rhythms, 60-61
    speech, 43-45
    stepping in rhythm, 43
    visualizing, 105
Rhythm instruments,
    hula hoop activities, 95
    introducing, 88
    nicknames, 182
    pretend instruments, 88
    putting away, 119
    strumming techniques, 88
    teaching strategies, 42
Rig A Jig Jig, 120
Rockin' Body Rhythms, 61-62

S

School song, 13
Scope and sequence of music, 97, 145
Self concept
    individual learning potential, 4
    personal learning power, 3
    self concept as a predicter of learning success, 3
    strong points, recognizing, 4
Self concept, ways of achieving
    changing concept of "family," recognizing, 10
    child's written self-revalation, 5
    children's names in songs, 106
    constructive criticism, 9, 11
    developing pride, 5
    encouragement vs. praise, 8
    eye contact, 10
    incorrect responses, 10

individual responses to a group question, 6
invite children's participation, 9
learning children's names, 185
music bulletin board, 184
music folder, 37
sending notes home, 8, 193
using students to demonstrate specific musical
    skills, 6
word choice, 9
See also *Atmosphere in the music class*
Simple behavior interventions
    peace bond, 29
    playing instruments out of turn, 28
    secret signal, 28
    solution table, 29
    student chatter, 28
    students' attention, regaining, 99, 100
    talking out of turn, 29, 94
    villain music, 89
Singing
    encouraging solo singing, 91
    mirror, using to teach singing, 96
    producing a good sound, 103
    singing in tune, 62, 95, 107
    visualization, 89
Style, strategies for teaching
    comparing styles, 71
    contrasting styles, 72
    elements of style, 72
    historical style periods, 72
    sample questions to ask, 71
Substitute teachers, 37
Symbols, *See Interpretive Symbols and Terms*

T

Talent Show
    all-school talent show, 198-199
    description, 91
    mini-talent show, 193
Teaching strategies
    beat strategies, 39-40
    concept chart, 35
    dynamics strategies, 73-76
    form strategies, 82-83
    giving instructions, 100
    harmony strategies, 67-69
    interpretive symbols and terms strategies, 83-85
    melody strategies, 59-67
    meter strategies, 51-60
    movement and direction strategies, 81-82
    Musical Password, 113
    new concept, introducing, 113-114
    partners teaching partners, 36
    phrase strategies, 58-59
    power thoughts, 33
    Project Create, 36
    questioning strategies, 35
    rhythm strategies, 41-50
    scope and sequence of music, 97
    style strategies, 71-72
    teacher talk, 35
    tempo strategies, 70-71
    tone color strategies, 77-81
    whole group instruction, 35
    whole group movement, 35
    new songs, teaching, 139-144
Tempo, strategies for teaching
    applause to teach, 102

establishing the tempo, 71
heartbeat, 70
hidden metronome, 114
metronome, 70
musical terms, 70
posters, 70
speed of heartbeats, 90
wind-up toys, 93
Terms, *See Interpretive Symbols and Terms*
Thinking skills
    developing, 19, 104
    rewarding, 19
Time away place, 22
Tone color, strategies for teaching
    clapping, 104
    games, 79
    imaginary instruments, 81, 184
    listening skills, developing, 77-78
    Musical Place Settings, 79
    Pop Bottle Symphony, 78
    rhythm instruments, 77
    vocal tone color, 80
Tune-a-grams, 13, 202

U

Unique New York, 133

V

Videotaping lessons, 37
Vocal warm-ups
    accurate pitch perception, 134
    diction, 132
    focus, 130
    harmony, 135-138
    open vowels, 134
    range, 131

W

Warm-ups
    attitude warm-ups, 122
    breathing warm-ups, 127-129
    motor warm-ups, 81, 123-125
    posture warm-ups, 124
    reasons for, 121
    selecting warm-ups for children, 121
    vocal warm-ups, 130-138
Whole-group activities
    behavior management, 20
    body jives, 115
    circle, forming a, 92
    daily chart, 20-21
    entering the room, 115
    evaluation, 101, 165-177
    going from standing to sitting, 92
    individual awards, 21
    instruction, 35
    lining up, 117, 119-120
    meter jives, 115
    most improved behavior award, 21
    movement, 35, 100
    regaining students' attention, 100
    remembering place, young children, 92
    response to questions, 63
    rewards, 19

BIBLIOGRAPHY

Andress, Barbara & Boardman, Eunice, *The Music Book*, New York, NY: Holt, Rinehart and Winston, 1984

Briggs, Dorothy, *Your Child's Self-Esteem*, Garden City, NY: Doubleday and Company, 1970.

Buscaglia, Leo, Ph.D., *Living, Loving and Learning*, New York, NY: Holt, Rinehart and Winston, 1982

Carnegie, Dale, *How to Win Friends and Influence People*, New York, NY: Pocket Books, 1981

Choksy, Lois, *The Kodaly Method*, Englewood Cliffs, NJ: Prentice-Hall, Inc., 1974

Elkind, David, *Miseducation*, New York, NY: Alfred A. Knopf, 1988

Fay, Jim & Cline, Foster & Shaw, Don, *Parenting With Love and Logic — A First Aid Kit for Parents*, Golden, CO: Cline/Fay Institute, 1986

Fay, Jim & Geddes, Betsy & Richard, Lyle & Funk, David, *The High Risk Student*, Golden, CO: School Consultant Services, Inc., 1990

Johnson, David W. & Roger T., *Learning Together and Alone*, Englewood Cliffs, NJ: Prentice-Hall, 1975

Lavender, Cheryl & Olsen, Joanne & Telleen, Charlotte, *Staging a Children's Musical*, Milwaukee, WI: Jenson Publications, Inc., 1987

Lewis, Aden G., *Listen, Look and Sing*, Glenview, IL: Silver Burdett Company, 1983

Mental Health Association in Waukesha County, Inc., *Self-Esteem*, Waukesha, WI: Mental Health Association in Waukesha County, Inc. and Community Human Services, 1989

Peck, M. Scott, M.D., *The Road Less Travelled*, New York, NY: Simon and Schuster, 1978

Roehmann, Franz L. & Wilson, Frank R., *The Biology of Music Making — Proceedings of the 1984 Denver Conference*, St. Louis, MO: MMB Music, Inc., 1988

Roehmann, Franz L. & Wilson, Frank, R., *Music and Child Development — Proceedings of the 1987 Denver Conference*, St. Louis, MO: MMB Music, Inc., 1990

Suzuki, Shinichi, *Nurtured by Love*, Smithtown, NY: Exposition Press, 1983

ABOUT THE
AUTHOR

CHERYL LAVENDER

Cheryl Ann Lavender is a music educator, author, clinician and composer. She is currently in her fifth year as an elementary music specialist in the Elmbrook School District, Brookfield, Wisconsin. Having been employed as a music educator over the past 17 years in school districts throughout Michigan and Wisconsin, her prior teaching experiences include vocal music instruction to pre-schoolers, elementary students, and junior high through high school students. A challenge and a highlight has been the implementation of comprehensive music education programs in three schools where none had existed. Cheryl also teaches private voice and piano.

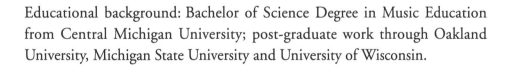

Having authored 17 publications since 1986, which include whole-group, musical-learning games and activities as well as resource collections for music educators, Cheryl freelances as a clinician, presenting topics such as: "Making Each Minute Count" (techniques which maximize musical learning in minimum class time), "Hop, Skip and a Heartbeat" (early-childhood musical strategies), and "Correlating Music and Language Arts' (a whole-language approach to elementary music education). Cheryl's works are published through Hal Leonard Publishing Corporation, Milwaukee, Wisconsin.

Educational background: Bachelor of Science Degree in Music Education from Central Michigan University; post-graduate work through Oakland University, Michigan State University and University of Wisconsin.

Personal background: from Detroit, Michigan; currently resides in Brookfield, Wisconsin, with husband Paul, and their three children.